THE BAYOU
STRANGLER

THE BAYOU STRANGLER

Louisiana's Most Gruesome Serial Killer

FRED ROSEN

OPEN ROAD

INTEGRATED MEDIA

NEW YORK

All rights reserved, including without limitation the right to reproduce this book or any portion thereof in any form or by any means, whether electronic or mechanical, now known or hereinafter invented, without the express written permission of the publisher.

Copyright © 2017 by Fred Rosen

Cover design by Mauricio Díaz

978-1-5040-3950-5

Published in 2017 by Open Road Integrated Media, Inc.
180 Maiden Lane
New York, NY 10038
www.openroadmedia.com

For my daughter, Sara, whose love and support during the writing of this book made it possible

CONTENTS

AUTHOR'S NOTE

This story is based on primary, on-the-scene reporting in the bayous of Louisiana; the investigative transcript of the case; and extended interviews with the primary detectives. Some names have been changed in the interest of privacy. But every single victim is as he was.

2017

Some stories take longer to come together than others. This is one of them. That it's about the serial killer who killed more victims than any other serial killer in the United States during the past two decades, well, you'd think that would have been enough to generate books, movies-of-the-week, films, TV-magazine broadcasts, and podcasts.

But that didn't happen. The sexuality of the killer and his choice of victims got in the way.

I've written four books about serial killers. This is the fifth. What I have discovered is that when the victims are prostitutes, society, including law enforcement, really doesn't care that much about them. But supposing the serial killer is *gay* and he targets *gay* men, most of whom are sex workers? That is rare.

Media outlets stayed away from the specifics of this story, of which there are many. One would hope that the sexuality of the bad guy and the victims wouldn't make any difference. But it does when it comes to press coverage, which always reflects public perceptions. If the serial killings also happen in Louisiana, the state with the highest per capita murder rate, who would care? What's one more victim in Louisiana to the media, let alone twenty-three?

I don't look at Louisiana as the murder capital of the United States. It's the place where, as a teenager, I had turtle soup and Shrimp Creole Agnew (named after the corrupt vice president who served President Richard Nixon) at Brennan's, one of New Orleans' best restaurants, and where I once made the mistake of ordering a drink called a hurricane in the French Quarter. It put me on the floor!

During that and subsequent trips, I discovered that no other state has Louisiana's unique DNA in its gumbo and étouffée. Louisiana has very heavy French, African, Spanish, Native American, and French Canadian influences, helping to account for its Cajun character. The state has a one-of-a-kind parish system, with really exotic names, instead of counties. Yet despite all of these unique cultural influences, there is a supposition in the northern and western parts of the United States that Southern cops are prejudiced.

In the late 1960s, this stereotype was best exemplified by Rod Steiger's Oscar-winning portrayal of Sheriff Bill Gillespie in *In the Heat of the Night*. During the 1970s, Clifton James, as the stocky, loud, and blustering Sheriff J. W. Pepper, faced off opposite Sir Roger Moore's first and second turns as 007 in *Live and Let Die* and *The Man with the Golden Gun*. James Best, one of television's finest character actors, took over the stereotype's mantle as Sheriff Roscoe Coltrane in *The Dukes of Hazzard*, which ran from 1979 to 1985.

On the contrary, nothing could be further from the truth.

The detectives on the case of the century's worst serial killer were anything but ignorant, racist idiots. Central casting would have a problem with this one. The Southern detectives on this case have advanced college degrees, allied with street smarts and a healthy lack of prejudice toward gay men.

There were in particular two detectives, a man and woman, who were willing to spend years of their lives hunting the bad guy—literally hunting the serial killer through two millennia—in order to bring justice and humanity to each and every one of his twenty-three victims. That is a story that had gotten lost—until now.

Never before have I seen such dedication to justice. Dennis Thornton and Dawn Bergeron truly speak for the dead.

THE BAYOU
STRANGLER

"There is no hunting like the hunting of man, and those who have hunted armed men long enough and liked it, never care for anything else thereafter."
—Ernest Hemingway

Walt Disney World, Orlando, Florida, 2006

Why do serial killers always seem to have a middle name or initial? Detective Dawn Bergeron knew the answer to that one.

It's because the arrest warrant, a legal document that a judge signs off on, always contains the killer's *full legal name*, including a middle name and/or middle initial, if there is one. But before you can get a warrant, you need a suspect. Or suspects.

His big black feet clomping, Mickey Mouse strode by on his way to a character breakfast, which cost a little bit more than regular admission. Bergeron was more than happy to give her daughter, Justine, a special breakfast on their vacation at Disney World.

Bergeron was wearing what she usually wore away from the job—jeans, a T-shirt, and black and brown Doc Martens. At work, she dressed more formally, in a pantsuit and blouse. Despite the Doc Martens, business had found her. Bergeron's business was homicide.

She had borrowed the Disney computer to check in on what was happening with her most pressing case. She opened an email from her task-force partner, Lieutenant Dennis Thornton of Jefferson Parish, fifty-eight miles from Terrebonne Parish, where Bergeron worked. Mickey Mouse would have blushed if he could have seen the arrest warrants for murder she was downloading from the email attachments that Thornton had sent to her.

Thornton has been on this case longer than anybody, she thought.

She began signing the forms that would, at last, bring the two-millennia-spanning manhunt to a close. Bergeron regularly worked out of the major crimes and juvenile division of the Terrebonne Parish Sheriff's Office, in the southern part of Louisiana on the Gulf of Mexico. Tall, curvy, and Southern Louisiana beautiful with tawny skin and high cheekbones, her horn-rimmed glasses could not disguise the slightly dark and exotic look of Bergeron's French relatives; you could see it in her eyes.

Her T-shirt swelled over large, voluminous breasts with a tattoo on the left breast that was only visible if she wore something extremely low-cut, which she seldom did. She had learned that it was the confidence built up in a suspect that made them talk. Big breasts were too distracting; at work, the jacket helped.

Bergeron was angry. She had wanted to cancel the vacation. She hadn't seen much point in going if they were close to finally arresting the serial killer, but she felt she owed it to her daughter. It had been a long haul; she and Thornton had been working twenty-two-hour days. Louisiana is a poor state; the task force didn't even have enough money for their overtime.

Instead, they'd surveilled the killer on their own time. They even let him know they were on his trail. With that much attention on him, he no longer had carte blanche to kill.

A real Disney World vacation would be good, she'd thought, no matter the results of the pending Sutterfield DNA tests. So she had gone, with assurance that nothing would happen until she returned. Wrong! But it was a "good" wrong. They had just gotten two mitochondrial-DNA hits from victim Oliver LeBanks. The semen in his rectum had been genetically linked to their prime suspect. Yet still they hesitated to pick up their killer.

Usually taken from a suspect's hair, mitochondrial DNA can only narrow the suspect down genetically to a given family. The results are therefore impeachable in court by a good defense attorney. What was needed for an airtight conviction at trial was a match of nuclear DNA. Nuclear DNA includes much more of the individual's genome or genetic makeup. A direct match. Nonetheless, the results convinced the department to begin round-the-clock surveillance on the suspect. The hope for a Sutterfield match was a nuclear-DNA hit.

"It's mitochondrial," Thornton told Bergeron over the phone, not hiding the disappointment in his voice.

"Well, what are we gonna do?" Bergeron asked the senior detective.

Thornton had spent eight years hunting the suspected killer when they finally found him in Bayou Blue. They discussed it for a while. If they arrested the guy now, they had a strong case to bring to trial, but not by any means a guaranteed conviction. But *not* to bring him into custody risked further homicides.

"We gotta pick him up," Thornton finally said. "Let's roll the dice."

Bergeron's daughter, Justine, had been looking forward to the vacation and was having a wonderful time. Like so many other times though, work interfered. They had bought seven-day passes. To add insult to injury, Disney doesn't give refunds. But maybe in this case . . .

Walt Disney had produced the first-ever television miniseries about serial killers!

In *Davy Crockett and the River Pirates* (1956), a sequel to the Davy Crockett miniseries, Davy Crockett (Fess Parker) and his pal Georgie Russell (Buddy Ebsen) raced riverboat-king Mike Fink (Jeff York) down the Ohio River to New Orleans. Then, in a twist based upon legend, Davy Crockett and Georgie Russell went up against Big Harpe and Little Harpe, America's first-known serial killers.

It would be nice to know if Walt Disney would have made an exception and given a refund to the detective about to arrest the new millennium's most prolific serial killer.

It was a little easier for Bergeron and her daughter to get back home to Louisiana than it had been for Davy and Georgie to get back to Tennessee, sailing up the Mississippi. Instead, Bergeron and her child left Frontier Land and flew back to New Orleans, and from there drove up to Houma. Bergeron dropped off Justine with a friend and then drove her white Dodge Charger over to the big stone slab of a building in the middle of town that served as headquarters for the Terrebonne Parish Sheriff's Office.

Walking up the steps, she thought about the victims. She'd thought about them a lot over the years the serial killer had been active. Twenty-three bodies strewn like so much detritus across Southern Louisiana. A lot of things needed to be explained. Until they got the killer into the interview room, it was hard to say what they would get from him.

Boy, she and Thornton really wanted to get this guy.

PART ONE

THE CLOAK OF NIGHT

CHAPTER ONE

THE QUARTERS

Orleans Parish, October 3, 1998

It all started eight years earlier, on the kind of day when you needed to take a shower to get dry. That's how hot and humid it was.

The unusually high temperature in the low eighties and the 80 percent humidity made it very uncomfortable. Ronald J. Dominique's damp T-shirt clung to his back. He did not rate a second glance from any of the hustlers, tourists, pickpockets, addicts, and strippers crowded into the streets of the French Quarter.

Short and stocky, five feet five inches tall and 160 pounds, he had a straggly black mustache and an unkempt black goatee on the lower part of his thin lips. Puffy cheeks and deep-set green eyes rounded out the picture of just another anonymous, slightly overweight, balding thirty-six-year-old American strolling through the French Quarter at twilight.

Dominique thought of the neighborhood as "the quarters."

To get out of the house, he had started going to the quarters. It was a good place. The trumpet notes of New Orleans jazz drifted out of the clubs onto Bourbon Street. He liked the music, though it did nothing to relax him. He went into a few of the raunchier clubs and tried a few draft beers. They didn't take the edge off either.

Sex. He needed sex.

There was something else that he couldn't easily define, something he felt that was more basic and that, even had he tried, he couldn't give words to. It just was time to troll. That's why he had parked his car, outside the quarters in a dark spot and gotten it ready. Inside his car, he had placed what he needed to satisfy his insatiable craving.

I know what I want. I need a guy to play around with, Dominique thought.

He knew that he wasn't an attractive man. Even when he did his Patti LaBelle impersonation all dressed up as the singer, nobody liked him. Making friends had never been easy. He'd also never had a long-term relationship with another man. It wasn't for lack of trying, but just as when he had been growing up, Dominique was laughed at, called a slob, a fag, a loser.

This wasn't San Francisco. Louisiana is a lot more conservative and, like many places in the United States, had not been so accepting of a gay man trying to come to grips with his sexuality. Dominique may have looked roly-poly, but that belied his strong upper body.

Trolling or fishing requires bait that attracts the fish to the hook. It's a simple, businesslike proposition. He had learned early on that it was easy in Southern Louisiana to buy sex. Lots of people did. Oliver LeBanks knew it too. And LeBanks also needed something—money.

The twenty-seven-year-old would sometimes pickpocket a tourist, maybe sell some drugs, or just hustle. No strong-arm stuff. Just a little bit here and there to make ends meet. Like Dominique, he had been strolling through the French Quarter enjoying himself, his brother and a couple gay friends by his side.

"I don't get it," said his brother. "What you with these guys for?"

"There are these old guys that like young guys like us. This is a way to make extra money," LeBanks explained reasonably. He was a businessman, about to make a proposition.

LeBanks, his brother, and his friends later went to 740 Burgundy, the location of Rawhide, a local gay bar popular with hustlers. With its constant flow of tourists, Rawhide was a great place to hustle sex, the kind of gay bar most gay bars fantasize about being. It was known as a leather-and-Levi's place where older guys cruised younger guys.

Time to get to work.

Throwing the door open, the music and boisterous laughter hit LeBanks like a hurricane. A jukebox in the back was blaring out some Patti LaBelle song. LeBanks's close-set dark eyes adjusted to the dim, smoky interior. He saw a pool table with guys using their cues to bang the balls into the holes.

On the right was the long teak and mahogany bar that curved around the room. The walls were decorated with multicolored license plates from all over the United States. Three sets of two supporting wooden pillars, six in all, were staggered down the bar, seeming to hold the whole place up. In practice, they divided the bar into cozy warrens of six-man sections, where intimate conversation and other mature things were possible.

It was already crowded-to-overflowing, with shirtless men sitting before cold bottles of beer. Many were middle-aged with paunches hanging down over their belts to their Bermuda shorts. There were a few men dressed in leather, brandishing whips with the idea of using them in ways Indiana Jones hadn't even thought of. However, for LeBanks, the place was the Temple of Doom.

The older leather boys mingled with younger guys in Levi's, boots, and Stetsons. LeBanks hung back a little, eying the customers at the bar, sizing them up. The upside down U-shaped aluminum handrails reflected the occasional flash of a tourist snapping a picture. LeBanks's friends took their shirts off to join in. He noticed a guy at the bar who wanted to blend in but could not.

Dominique wasn't about to expose himself in public, not with his portly frame. Too embarrassing; he'd had enough of that. He was sick and tired of his family ridiculing him for being gay. Their taunts made him ashamed at first, and then angry.

He kept his shapeless T-shirt on, figuring the money in his pocket would do the talking when the time was right. He kept busy drinking a cold bottle of Purple Haze, an American-style wheat beer with a slight raspberry taste that was lost on Dominque that night.

Dominique was too busy thinking about other things, like the slim black guy who sat down in the empty stool next to his, ordered a beer, and started to talk to him. After a few minutes of chitchat, the hustler got down to business.

"You like to have a good time?" LeBanks asked, drinking his beer casually.

"I like to fool around," Dominique replied.

His Southern Louisiana accent betrayed him to LeBanks as a native. Probably from up in the Houma area. That part of Terrebonne Parish was crisscrossed with bayous, a rural place centered around a small town. Locals referred to the town as "up," though in fact it was fifty-five miles southwest of New Orleans.

But that made no difference. Local was all right with LeBanks. Money was money.

"Sure," LeBanks said.

"I ain't got no money for no motel or nothing," Dominique explained.

"I don't have none either," answered LeBanks.

Dominique had a ready solution: instant intimacy that had worked for many couples since Henry Ford had invented the Model T automobile in 1908.

"Come on, we'll go to my vehicle. It's parked nearby. You need money?" Dominique asked.

LeBanks knew what the guy wanted. He'd done it before. There was only one more thing that needed to be said.

"How much you got?"

"About twenty or thirty dollars," Dominique responded.

The price was fine with LeBanks. That was the rate for a blow job. Sounded good. It was a business transaction, plain and simple: step out to do it, and then come back to make some more money with some other guys. Names weren't needed; just cash.

"Why don't we go to my car? It's parked right near here," said Dominique, slipping off the bar stool.

LeBanks eyed him again. He saw nothing out of the ordinary—green eyes and round, placid face. Dressed in jeans and a T-shirt, Dominique looked like any other guy wanting to get his rocks off on a handsome young hustler like LeBanks. Dominique led the way out. Outside, they turned down St. Ann Street and continued walking.

If LeBanks had been paying attention, the first tip-off would have been that the guy's car wasn't as close as he'd said it was. They had to keep walking through the pools of light that distinguished the Quarter, past the old balconied buildings that were young in corsair Jean Lafitte's time. Lafitte had been known as the "Pirate Patriot."

Without Lafitte and his pirates fighting alongside him, General Andrew Jackson—Old Hickory—would have lost the Battle of New Orleans, where he defeated the English in 1815. Dominique and LeBanks passed Lafitte's old blacksmith shop on Bourbon Street, where he and his brother had first started their criminal enterprises.

The men walked out of the Quarter, to quiet, dark side streets where shadowy hulks were parked by the curb.

"I'm over here," Dominique gestured, "where that new shopping thing by the Jax Brewery is."

It was late and the parking lot next to the Jax Brewery was mostly empty. Dominique opened up the back door of a ten-year-old tan Chevy Malibu station wagon, with a luggage rack on top. Dominique got in and LeBanks piled in on top of him. He was all ready to go, really wanting some action.

Dominique watched as LeBanks pulled off his T-shirt, exposing a muscular torso. Dominique stripped down quickly, pulling his pants and what he thought of as his "drawers" all the way down. Not wasting any time, LeBanks went down on him. LeBanks sucked Dominique's penis until Dominique twisted LeBanks around so that they sucked each other simultaneously.

"Now lay on your stomach," Dominique instructed.

He had not negotiated for that; fucking would be more. But before LeBanks could say anything else, Dominique got on top of him, his weight crushing him down on the seat.

"I was hurt before. I was split," said Dominique.

The comment had no context to LeBanks because he wasn't a mind reader. He didn't know that Dominique had been raped, and how determined he was to never have that happen again. With LeBanks struggling to get out from under the big man's weight, Dominique pushed his penis into the man's rectum. LeBanks protested he was being hurt, but Dominique was relentless. He pushed harder and harder and harder, until finally he ejaculated.

"Now get on top of me and rub your thing on me," Dominique ordered.

LeBanks got on top of Dominique and began rubbing his penis against the guy's flabby ass. Dominique thought he felt some penetration. And that was it.

"You was just supposed to rub it."

He'd had enough, and he'd been forced to put up with too much to stop there. The ridicule, the stone glances from his family, and now just *thinking* someone was about to violate him again made him want, *finally, to* do something about it. It was an intoxicating combination of fear and retribution. And he had prepared for just such an eventuality.

Reaching down to the floorboards, he felt the cold metal of the tire iron in his strong hand. He brought it up quickly and slammed it into the side of Oliver LeBanks's head. He brought up the iron and hit him again. As the smaller man's brain began leaking out blood inside his cranium, the struggle seeped out of him. His limbs stopped pushing, then twitched, finally going slack.

Physicians call it a concussion. Unless LeBanks were operated on immediately, the twin concussions he had sustained when the tire iron impacted his head would soon kill him. Dominique showed no mercy. He got on top of LeBanks and began to choke him.

Already unconscious from the blows, LeBanks started twitching again, and then Dominique heard the death rattle, the last gasp of the life that he had just violated. He took off his belt, wrapped it around the now unmoving figure. Putting his weight on top of him again, Dominique pulled the belt tight, so it bit into LeBanks's skin.

After a while—Dominique wasn't sure how long it was—he realized the guy was once and for all not breathing anymore. He threw open the back door and jumped out of the station wagon into the deserted street. Dominique had killed before. He knew what he had to do. He got into the driver's seat, fished his keys out of his pocket, plunged the key into the ignition, and started up the car.

CHAPTER TWO

OUTSIDE THE BOX

Dominique began driving down dark streets, not really knowing where he was, looking for the right place to dump the body. He'd know when he saw it. He wound up driving into Kenner, the oldest city in Jefferson Parish, established in 1855. Back then, the place was known by its French name, Cannes Brûlées (burnt cane fields).

It was a landmark on the banks of the Mississippi River. The family of its founder, William Kenner, owned many of the area's larger plantations and farms. Everything changed in 1915 when a commuter rail line was established from Kenner to New Orleans, bringing in manufacturing. That, in turn, brought in new roads and the airports.

A full-fledged suburb, Kenner was connected to the Big Easy by Interstate 10, the major east/west interstate in the southern United States. Interstate 10 goes all the way from Jacksonville, Florida, on the Atlantic Ocean, across the southwestern United States, terminating at Santa Monica on the Pacific Ocean in California.

A few miles north of the busy New Orleans International Airport, Dominique turned his tan Malibu wagon south. He took a left down Airport Road. As he circled the airport looking for a location that he would know instinctively was right, the overhead jets had a bird's-eye view of his travels.

Too many people, too many cars; the place was just too active. What had he been thinking? No place to do it that wouldn't be easily found. But that was part of the kick for Dominique. *It couldn't be too easy, he wanted the body to be found.* Had he not, he could have easily just gone over a bridge and dumped it into some dark waters.

Or he could have driven to a nearby bayou and let the alligators take care of things, neatly and tastily, without leaving a trace for a forensic specialist to work with. It just wouldn't scratch that itch inside him if he did that. What fun would it be? What pleasure it would give him when the body was found!

The body had to be found.

He was sick and tired of people not giving him credit for things. Now he'd show them. He'd killed again and the body would be proof. *Proof.*

He took a left onto Airline Drive, also known as Federal Highway 61. Heading east, back toward New Orleans, he passed the Hilton and Lexington hotels again, their entrances lit up like it was Christmas. Dominique was one of those people who loved Christmas all year round. He kept Christmas decorations up full-time in his trailer. But this wasn't the holiday season. Those lights meant people were around, people who might see him and what he was doing, what he had done.

Again, too busy, too many people driving in and out. No, that wouldn't do, and he kept going.

He passed food management and construction offices. Airline Drive is host to a variety of businesses that cater to the airline traveler going through New Orleans. After a few miles, Airline Drive passed into the town of Metairie (pronounced MET-ur-ee).

Dominique saw Providence Memorial Park Cemetery on his right, where Mahalia Jackson, the celebrated gospel singer, had been laid to rest. But he was hardly into gospel. Leaving Mahalia and the cemetery behind him, he continued east toward New Orleans, still on Airline Drive, passing the fast food and chain restaurants, gas stations, and strip malls that dotted the highway.

Passing Little Farms Avenue, he approached Dickory Avenue. Just past the light at the intersection of Dickory Avenue and the end of the Earhart Expressway was a speed trap. Waiting for speeders at the bottom of the elevated highway was Louisiana state trooper Cal Calhoun. His job was to catch and ticket speeders, who would not see his car hidden in a parking lot at the bottom of the exit ramp.

Obeying the speed limit as he always did, Dominique drove right past the cop. Dickory Avenue rose as it got to the six-thousand block of Stable Drive before hitting the railroad tracks. Below Stable was a feeder road into Zephyr Field a quarter of a mile east, where the Triple-A New Orleans Zephyrs minor-league team played its home games.

There was nothing special about the overpass except that it was conveniently there, secluded but accessible to passersby. Perfect for dumping a body. The tan Malibu wagon tooled down Stable Drive, deserted at this hour. Dominique pulled the wagon to the side of the road, hopped out, went around to the passenger-side door, and threw it open.

Pulling LeBanks's corpse by the belt still wrapped around its neck, he struggled until he had it fully out under the overpass. Then he let it go. The body plunked down on the sand, face down. Cutting back quickly to the station wagon, Dominique closed the rear passenger-side door, which made a hollow sound in the empty darkness.

Getting back behind the wheel, he turned the ignition on and put the car into drive. A moment later, Ronald J. Dominique was well away, driving the few blocks north to Airline Drive. This time, he didn't circle the airport, but kept going. Ten miles down the road, he saw the interstate looming overhead.

Interstate 310 is a freeway linking US 90 and Southern Louisiana to Interstate 10 and metropolitan New Orleans. He turned right up the ramp, then took a left and headed southwest. In seven miles, the road climbed higher and passed over the Mississippi River, providing Dominique with a great view of the Big Muddy flowing below him.

On the other side, the road passed over Westbank Bridge Park and curved south. In front of him were two signs. The one for the right lane said "90 West, Houma," while the one for the left said "90 East, Boutte, New Orleans." Dominique followed the sign to Boutte, at the southern end of the roadway. He turned north on the Old Spanish Trail, pulling off at the trailer park where he lived.

Trailers were everywhere. Some were set on wooden foundations, some on concrete; some had gardens in front; and some were really modular homes. The one thing they had in common: anonymity.

The next day, a passerby saw the body below the freeway ramp and called the police. Because the corpse had been dumped in Jefferson Parish, the lead homicide investigator from the sheriff's office was summoned to the scene. If it should turn out that the victim was killed in, say, Terrebonne Parish, the latter would then assume venue, but for now, Jefferson was up at bat.

This guy is sloppy, thought Dennis Thornton. *Otherwise, how come we find a fresh body?*

Dressed like a banker in charcoal-gray suit, blue tie, and wing-tipped shoes, Detective Lieutenant Dennis Thornton bent over and examined the partially clothed body of the man he would eventually identify as Oliver LeBanks.

Murder was a much more frequent occurrence in Louisiana than in other places, and therefore, not unusual. Louisiana and in particular the New Orleans metropolitan area has the highest per capita homicide rate in the country. Sorting through the similarities and differences between so many homicides can be a daunting task.

Linkage. It was all about linkage in serial-killer cases. Do that and you'd save lives. Link homicides to the same perpetrator and concentrate your resources there. It was an inviolable clock, ticking away the life-seconds of the next victims.

Thornton looked up at the jets flying overhead. The airport was nearby. *Did the killer live near the airport?* he wondered.

Yes, he did. But what Thornton didn't know was that the killer was closer than anyone realized. And LeBanks had *not* been his first victim. The first had been David Mitchell, a nineteen-year-old African American, who was last seen on July 13, 1997, in St. Charles Parish. That's right up Interstate 310, not far from where Dominique was living in Boutte.

Mitchell's fully clothed body was discovered the day after his disappearance on Louisiana Highway 3160, off Highway 18 in an industrial area of the parish. He had been anally raped before being drowned.

Dominique next struck exactly five months later to the day, again close to home.

Gary Pierre, a twenty-year-old African American, was found dead on December 14 in St. Charles Parish. The coroner ruled that Pierre had been murdered "by asphyxiation, due to neck compression." He too had been raped.

Serial killers can change patterns. Sometimes they have a cooling-off period between crimes. Dominique seemed to be one of those. Consistent to his pattern, at least for the moment, Dominique once again took a vacation from killing, this time for seven months. Then Larry Ranson showed up.

Like Mitchell and Pierre, he was African American and had last been seen in St. Charles. Ranson was thirty-eight years old. Dominique was changing his victim of choice, showing age wasn't a factor. Serial killers usually zero in on a type and remain constant.

Ranson's fully clothed body was discovered the day after he disappeared on July 31, off Louisiana 316 in an industrial area of the parish. The coroner later said Ranson's manner of death was "asphyxiation due to neck compression." Ranson would have been conscious the whole time he was being choked until, mercifully, he blacked out because his brain wasn't getting air and drifted into death.

Because the bodies had been dumped close to one another off the same road, the police in St. Charles suspected one killer. But the culprit had left nothing behind for the cops to work with—no fibers, no prints, no hair. The lack of DNA, plus the anal bruising of the victims, made the cops figure he was using a condom. They sorted through the usual list of parolees with charges of sexual abuse of one sort or another in their files, but came up with nothing.

What Southern Louisiana was unknowingly facing was a serial killer, and a successful one. Once a serial killing has been confirmed in a locality, the FBI is contacted and they make a profile of the killer. The profiles are generally cookie-cutter.

"The serial killer is white, poor, and doesn't have much of an education."

While that profile would certainly fit Dominique, it also fit a couple million other guys in Louisiana and would be of no practical use.

Solving a serial killing means thinking outside the box. Once in a while, a detective will get assigned to investigate and no matter where the trail leads, no matter how long it takes, the detective decides to dedicate part of his life to tracking down a murderer who had the audacity to kill in his parish. Dominique didn't know it, but he had made an enemy of Dennis Thornton.

Evidence markers were set up near tire imprints in the soft sand where LeBanks's body had been dumped. There was no evidence of a murder weapon. Examining the body, Thornton saw that the victim had been bludgeoned on one side of the head. The killer had left the pants of the victim down below his knees. His shirt was off.

Thornton wore surgical gloves to prevent contamination. Not that he was afraid the dead man could contaminate him; it was the other way around. The idea was that the detective bring nothing to the scene, including his own fingerprints, that could contaminate the evidence. Thornton picked up the wrists and noted the ligature or binding marks. It looked like the guy's wrists had been tied together. Thornton was going to be very interested in what the coroner had to say about them.

As the morgue attendants moved in with the bags, tarps, and collapsible table that formed the tools of their trade, Thornton stepped back to allow them to do their job.

You can never be sure how wrists are tied together until the coroner weighs in. And details like the pants around the victim's ankles could turn out to be the killer's signature behavior.

CHAPTER THREE

THE DETECTIVE

St. Charles, Jefferson, and Orleans Parishes,
December 15–30, 1998

The next day, like nothing special had happened, Ronald J. Dominique reported for work at the St. Charles Parish Maintenance Department. Dominique had already killed three times before. Picking up his shovel to begin his day's work, he was unaware that in neighboring Jefferson Parish, the coroner was picking up his scalpel.

Oliver LeBanks's naked body was laid out on the examining table in the morgue, all set for the "Y" incision that would expose his organs to the pathologist's blade. Dr. Harry Landers was ready to start cutting when Dennis Thornton stopped him. Detectives regularly attend autopsies to assist the coroner and to gather evidence. Thornton had noticed something.

"Look at the hairs," said Thornton. "Oliver has Caucasian hairs on his body."

Thornton was well suited to the job: a streetwise, intelligent, well-educated homicide investigator who knew his trade. He had a bachelor of science in criminal justice from Loyola University, which he followed up with graduate work at Indiana State University, earning a master of arts in criminology. And he treated everyone the same. Black, white, made no difference; all were people who deserved his best.

Thornton produced an evidence envelope. Using gloved hands and sterile tweezers, Landers began picking up the hairs and dropping them into the envelope in the detective's hand. It took a few minutes, because there were a lot of them. It was very clear when held up to the light that they were indeed Caucasian.

When Landers was finished, Thornton sealed and marked the envelope. The idea now was to maintain the chain of custody. The chain of custody is a record of individuals who have physical possession of the evidence. Maintaining it is vital. If evidence is contaminated by other DNA—from the people handling, it for example—it's the first thing a good defense attorney will attack in court to get their client off.

If police developed a prime suspect, they could try to match his DNA to those hairs. Thornton put the sealed evidence in his briefcase for safekeeping. When he got to the station, he'd log it in as evidence. Then it would be sent out to a private lab for testing.

The coroner picked up his scalpel again and this time went to work. The autopsy took less than an hour. When it was over, Landers had some answers for Dennis Thornton. LeBanks had been bludgeoned either before or after being bound (the ligature marks on the wrist), raped (deep anal bruising, but no semen, meaning the killer had used a condom), and strangled to death.

The coroner found hemorrhaging at the key points where the killer put his hands around Oliver LeBanks's neck. LeBanks, who had a record of low-level crimes, was easily identified by his fingerprints. With the help of the victim's family and friends, Thornton backtracked his movements on the day of his death. LeBanks's girlfriend, Judy Jason, who was really shaken up, and his brother, Michael LeBanks, were interviewed and given the details of his last night.

According to Judy and Michael, there was nothing out of the ordinary about LeBanks's movements that day prior to entering the Quarter, when he separated from his brother and went with his two gay friends into the "raw hole," as the cops called Rawhide.

Thornton drove his unmarked Chrysler into the Quarter and parked on Burgundy Street. Walking past a few storefronts, he came to Rawhide. Back in the day, *Rawhide* was a 1960s American-Western television series that made Clint Eastwood a star. Now, it was the gay bar from which Oliver LeBanks disappeared—until he turned up dead.

Unlike many police officers and prosecutors, who tended to dehumanize anyone engaging in prostitution, Thornton was a real pro; he refrained from judging the victim on the basis of his sexual orientation. *Who cares whether the victim was gay?* "Oliver" was how Thornton thought of him. He didn't care whether Oliver was hustling gay sex or not. He was a human being who got in way over his head and was murdered.

The detective saw that it was business as usual at Rawhide: leather, Bermuda shorts, beer, stroking, guys coming and going. Thornton stood out in his neat suit and tie. He moved into the bar, between bare-chested bikers, and questioned the bartenders, showing them a mug shot of LeBanks.

No one remembered him.

Working Burgundy Street outside, Thornton tried a few merchants, addicts, and prostitutes. No one had seen LeBanks on the street. Getting back into his car, Thornton found it remarkable that no one saw his body being dumped either, as though his killer had blended into thin air.

Thin air my ass!

Dennis Thornton knew that whoever this guy was, he hadn't bothered to cover his trail. He could have secreted the body, at least for a few more days until someone discovered it by chance. Yet he didn't do that. He had dumped LeBanks in a less populated area, but one that did see car traffic. The killer had seen the freeway and it looked convenient.

He may even, for some reason of his own, have wanted the body discovered.

Thornton knew the homicide statistics for the state, which consistently ranked in the top five in the nation for females murdered in single incidents, usually by men they knew. The killer he was tracking didn't fit into the latter category. The only thing he could conclude, so far, was that LeBanks's killer had acted alone. There was no evidence to show otherwise.

It looked like an ordinary hookup, probably a business deal—sex for money. Which might make the suspect gay.

Fifteen days after Oliver LeBanks was murdered, Joseph Brown turned up dead, his partially clothed body found on the western end of Veteran's Memorial Boulevard in Kenner. That gave venue to the detectives of St. Charles Parish, who soon discovered that Brown, an African American, was all of sixteen years old.

As for the method of death, the coroner concluded "death by asphyxiation, due to strangulation." The police had no other clues or leads to the killer. One month later, Bruce Williams became the next victim discovered. This time, the body was fully clothed, dumped in an industrial area of Jefferson Parish.

Again, Dennis Thornton got the call.

The details were the same as with LeBanks—he had been strangled and raped. Male-on-male rape was not a crime that police officers encountered often. Thornton saw the immediate similarities and his mind made the necessary linkage. Once again, he backtracked the victim's movements and, this time, he discovered that Williams, an eighteen-year-old African American, had been a hustler much like LeBanks, only he lived in New Orleans.

He had walked over to the French Quarter the night of November 27 and disappeared.

The parish reached out to the FBI for help. It wasn't Thornton's decision alone, of course. There were higher-ups who were captains, commanders, majors, whatever, who carried a lot more pull. But when a decision is finally reached internally that a serial killer is their quarry, calling in the FBI is firm policy across the country.

The FBI had conducted a serial-killer project in the 1970s. Their idea was to try to identify and analyze the most common characteristics of serial murderers, which could then be used to capture them. In our book *Tracker: Hunting Down Serial Killers*, my coauthor, Dr. Maurice Godwin, the renowned geographic profiler, writes: "With good intentions, the FBI proceeded, but unfortunately without scientific evaluation. FBI agents conducted interviews with thirty-six incarcerated men, only twenty-five of whom were serial killers."

The lack of a real scientific basis for the study didn't stop the bureau from developing what it termed the profiles of the "organized" and "disorganized" serial killer. It became the most widely used profiling "model" in the world. But because it was based on a specious study, the results came into question among criminologists during the 1980s.

Most local police departments that used the FBI's profiling services soon found they all got the same "white male, mid-thirties, high school dropout, difficulty with social skills" cookie-cutter profile. It was no different for Jefferson Parish. But the FBI narrowed the hunt down further for them. Based upon the string of dump sites, they had a possible location for the suspect.

"This guy lives near the airport," FBI profiler Tom Colby told Thornton.

Well, that narrowed it down to another million guys, thought Thornton.

But it did seem accurate. The guy had dumped bodies on both sides of the airport. Why in these places? Besides being sloppy—or maybe because of it—could he have wanted the bodies to be seen? As for where he lived, it did seem logical to Thornton that it would be nearby—but where?

Cookie-cutter or not, this time the FBI got it right. They didn't know it, but their profile fit Ronald J. Dominique exactly. Dominique lived in Boutte, just thirteen and a half miles from New Orleans International Airport. Of course it also fit millions of other guys in Louisiana and probably more than a few in the airport vicinity. But only one of them was a serial killer who decided, once again, to go trolling in the quarters at night.

Ronald J. Dominique was on the prowl for another male hustler who needed money. And he soon found him. His name was Manuel Reed. A native of the Big Easy, Reed was African American, twenty-one years old, with a slim muscular build that was evident when his partially clothed body was discovered inside a business dumpster in Kenner on May 30, 1999.

"Death by asphyxia due to strangulation," ruled the coroner. And like all the rest, Reed had been raped before he died.

While some serial killers do their killing across state lines, many, like Dominique, murder close to home. That proximity gives them a comfort zone, knowing that once the job is done, they can get away safely and easily and be home quickly. It was Angel Mejia, then, who changed the serial killer's paradigm.

Angel Mejia was a homeless, twenty-one-year-old African American. With no permanent address, he worked the streets for his existence. Last seen alive on the afternoon of June 30, 1999, he was found that night in front of a business dumpster in an industrial area of Kenner.

In front of the dumpster.

As Thornton viewed the body, he remembered what he had thought about the killer—he was sloppy and he was proving it again and again. Mejia was partially clothed and had been raped. "Death by asphyxia due to strangulation," the coroner wrote in his report. It was getting to be a rather repetitive—not to mention frustrating—line.

No matter what testing they did, they still could not come up with anything on the killer's prints, DNA, or even his car's tire impressions. They had those hairs, but no database to check them with, and, more importantly, no suspect to check them against. And even if you identified a suspect, you needed a search warrant to get his DNA, unless he consented.

Then, to make matters worse, the media got involved. *The Advocate* broke the story on June 23, 1999, with the sensationalistic headline:

SHOELESS BODY COULD BE WORK
OF SERIAL KILLER

"A serial killer may be responsible for the deaths of three young men, whose shoeless bodies were dumped in isolated areas around New Orleans International Airport over the past eight months," the article said. It was also mentioned that Angel Mejia and Joseph Brown "knew each other and had a history of dealing drugs."

Making a public statement that a serial killer is working in a specific locality is a double-edged sword that requires careful handling. On one hand, it allows people to be aware of what's happening and take measures to protect themselves. On the other hand, it lets the bad guy know the cops are on to him, thus giving him a chance to cover his tracks and run.

And so that's how the urban myth of the Shoeless Serial Killer was born. It has alliteration going for it. Local television stations went with it, claiming that all the serial killer's bodies had been missing their shoes. On the Internet, amateur sleuths who had never even heard of Mycroft Holmes claimed without substantiation that removing the shoes was part of this serial killer's *modus operandi* (MO), his *signature behavior*, the thing he did that made him unique. Mycroft Holmes's little brother, Sherlock, might have disagreed.

Thornton, too, knew that wasn't accurate. It just made good copy. In the cases where the shoes were missing, they were found nearby. In others, the victims were wearing shoes when the police found them. More revealing was who the victims were.

Street people, they led transient lives, here today gone tomorrow. They were people that would never be missed. Like Mitchell Johnson.

CHAPTER FOUR

THE SURE TIP-OFF

Terrebonne and Lafourche Parishes,
November 1–December 31, 1999

Mitchell Johnson was the kind of guy that Dominique liked to fuck and kill—a well-built thirty-four-year-old black man. Of course, Dominique didn't know his name; that didn't matter.

Johnson's body was dumped under the same overpass where LeBanks's had been discarded. Police found Johnson literally a few feet away from the exact spot where LeBanks had been discovered. Thornton was puzzled and enraged—it was as if the killer were playing a game. Perhaps he had seen or heard the reports of the investigation and was screwing with the heads of the posse that was after him?

Was the killer so supremely overconfident to the point of insanity, or was he purposely sloppy, hoping to get caught? Thornton didn't know yet. The autopsy report came back that Johnson, like the rest, had been raped and strangled. Same MO.

Witnesses said they last saw Johnson in Kenner; there was a suspicious guy cruising around about the same time Johnson disappeared.

Witnesses gave Thornton a rough description of a white male, mid-thirties, receding hairline, puffy cheeks. A police sketch artist produced a picture of the suspect. Was this the killer? The guy didn't look very dangerous, except maybe in the eyes. They seemed to just stare out at you, without registering any emotion.

Sketch in hand, the detective decided to reach out to both the mainstream and gay media in the New Orleans area. Given the fact that every victim was male and had been raped—a decidedly unusual MO—the police thought that the killer was targeting gays. In November 1999, the New Orleans *Times-Picayune*, the city's only big newspaper, published the sketch of the suspect, reporting that police were describing him as a serial killer targeting men in the area.

Later, officials wouldn't know whether Dominique had seen that article, or if it played any role in his decision to pick up and leave Boutte. But in November 1999, shortly after it was published, he quit his job with the county and drove his trailer home to Houma. Houma is only fifty-eight miles southwest of New Orleans, off of Interstate 90, next to the Gulf of Mexico. Boutte was a New Orleans suburb. Houma was way south.

Dawn Bergeron had already been in Houma for a decade. Her oilman father moved his family there when Bergeron was a teenager in the 1980s. Southern Louisiana's economy is dependent upon the oil rigs in the Gulf of Mexico, which pump up black gold and jobs. Lit up like a Christmas tree at night, the Deepwater Horizon was the biggest.

After high school, Bergeron went south to attend Louisiana State University in Baton Rouge, where she got her bachelor of arts in criminal justice in 1994. Moving back up to Houma, she joined the Terrebonne Parish Sheriff's Office. She could have joined the Houma Police Department, which had venue inside the actual city, but the sheriff's office roamed the entire parish and there was something appealing to Bergeron about that.

A deputy is a street cop working for the county, not the town or city. As a sheriff's deputy riding in a squad car, Bergeron quietly observed the type of crimes detectives are asked to investigate. Among them was sexual abuse, which she investigated as a member of the Sheriff's Homicide and Juvenile Division. The parish had a huge sex abuse rate, with a significant number of cases of parents sexually abusing their children.

Her education and demeanor placed her way above the average deputy sheriff in her county. Promoted to detective, Bergeron spent a lot of time in the interview room taking statements from parents who would claim they had sex with their child in the same way their parents had had sex with them. Parish detectives spoke privately about how some juvenile abuse came about as a result of Cajun culture. They said that some Cajuns accepted parents having sex with their children as the natural order of things.

Squad detectives were also called on to investigate homicides. Homicides usually fell into one run-of-the mill category or another, with the common motives of money, sex, and revenge. Learning her trade, Bergeron balanced her professional life with her private one. She married a cop and had a child. She had a funny, knowing laugh—which you need when you have to juggle warrants and child.

And then life in Houma changed when Ronald J. Dominique came back home from Boutte.

He drove down Broadway, past the town square, where more than a century earlier, the bodies of Union soldiers mutilated by

Southern guerrillas were left to rot in the sun. He took a left to go across one of the town's bridges, over the alligator infested bayous that cut right through the town.

Dominique went over to Bayou Blue Road, a long street, mostly rural, with cane fields and the occasional house bordering the highway. He turned in at one of them, his sister Lainie's place, and parked in the yard. There she and her husband welcomed him, allowing her brother to hook up his mobile home to the electricity and water in the yard.

People in the parish identified themselves by the road they lived on. That's how Dominique became a "Bayou Blue man," by settling at his sister's home on that road. Directly across the street was a church, its pale white paint peeling from the sun, the high humidity, and occasional hurricane. Dominique was a man on the run but no one, including his sister, knew that.

He was eager to assume an appearance of normalcy as soon as possible, lest anyone see the police sketch. However, it had not been distributed as widely as Dominique might have assumed. In fact, the Terrebonne Parish Sheriff's Office and Houma police had not been sent the sketch. Unless he made a mistake, Dominique was safe.

Little did anyone in Houma realize, a serial killer was now in their midst.

With the successful hookup to electricity and water, Dominique had all the comforts of home. Yet he needed a *second* trailer, which he would later put to good use. He bought a smaller, beat-up trailer that he parked next to the larger one. And, having to support himself, Dominique went to work as a laborer for Caro Produce on Brien Street.

This wasn't New York City, where men could walk around arm in arm and not rate a second look. This was Houma, Louisiana, where small, long lakes called bayous leak out into the

Gulf of Mexico. Dominique sought attention from a world that ridiculed him, at worst, for being gay, and at best, for being homely.

He did and said nothing to stand out. In conversations with people, he was nice and polite, his speech peppered with "Yes, ma'am" and "No, ma'am" like some Southern gentleman. People looked through him, like he didn't exist. In a sense, he didn't. Terrebonne Parish has a high rate of illiteracy. Many do not read the newspapers or watch television. They knew nothing about the Shoeless Serial Killer and his eight murders in the northern parishes.

Beneath Houma's sleepy Southern appearance was an undercurrent of abysmal poverty where people lived in shacks, couldn't afford cars or car insurance, and rode bicycles to get around. The town had exactly two gay bars and a slew of others where whatever beer was cheap or on special was the beverage of choice.

The poor residents lived on the fringes, in the shacks and apartments off the main streets of the town, bordering the bayou. Some lived farther out in the country. Wherever you were, one type of coyote or another roamed at night.

Michael Rydell Vincent was a young African American man who lived in a rundown apartment on Peters Street. He, like his killer, sported a mustache and a goatee. He'd been a criminal long enough to have an a.k.a. (also known as), which in his case was "Chris Vincent." Regardless of the name he used, Vincent was a small guy—five-foot-seven and 121 pounds soaking wet.

Despite his lack of size, or perhaps because of it, he'd been arrested for aggravated battery. His record indicated that he hustled sex with men, a record that came to an end when he vanished on New Year's Eve, 1999. The next day, a motorist on

Highway 7 in neighboring Lafourche Parish saw a body that had been dumped on a barbed wire fence right off the road.

The motorist made a police report, and detectives arrived to process the crime scene. Because of the holiday, the autopsy had to wait until everyone returned to work on the morning of January 3, 2000. The autopsy began at 8:20 a.m. in the coroner's office in Jefferson Parish. Dr. Susan M. Garcia was the forensic pathologist in charge. She also had two assistants from the coroner's office, Detectives Chad Shelby and Jason Fanguy of the Lafourche Parish Sheriff's Office.

During the external examination, Garcia noted that Vincent had been wearing blue jeans, blue boxer underwear, white socks, a white T-shirt, and a reddish-green long-sleeved plaid shirt. Inside the right front pocket Garcia found a key ring with two keys. In the right pants pocket were four pieces of crack, the deadly, addictive, and relatively cheap cocaine derivative.

Dr. Garcia placed the drugs, keys, and loose change in evidence envelopes, which she turned over to Shelby and Fanguy. Then Garcia got to the heart of it. She noted two linear abrasions on the right upper chest crossing the right breast, two superficial cuts on the lower right side, and a small superficial scrotal abrasion.

She saw the ligature marks on Michael Vincent's wrists. Garcia looked at Vincent's brown eyes and noted "fine pinpoint conjunctival petechiae bilateral and one coalescent focus of sclerotic hemorrhage on the right." Petechiae are red dots under the skin caused by capillaries that have leaked. There can be many medical reasons for this kind of condition, including autoimmune disorder, viral infections, bone marrow disorder, and bloodstream infections.

If you ruled out all of those natural reasons, petechiae is a sure tip-off to strangulation. The condition occurs when the vessels burst in the eye due to pressure on the throat. The burst capillaries then cause the red dots under the eye tissue.

Examining the mouth, Garcia saw that Vincent had one solid-gold-capped tooth. The rest of his teeth were in fairly good condition. Vincent had been lucky that way. Dental care was not exactly the most important thing in a street hustler's milieu. He certainly didn't have dental insurance and neither did the people he hung out with.

The pathologist used her scalpel to open the body and a saw to take off the skullcap, in the usual autopsy fashion. She noted no brain abnormalities or hemorrhaging. As for the trunk, there were no abnormal fluid accumulations in any body cavity. That meant no internal bleeding from beatings, guns, knives, or anything else.

Finishing her examination, the coroner saw a tattoo of the letters "E.O.G." on the back of the right hand, and a tattoo with the name "Vincent" on the back of the left hand. Garcia concluded her findings as follows: "DIAGNOSES – Circumstances surrounding death are unclear but subtle findings at autopsy suggested that homicidal asphyxia is the cause of death. Manner of death is homicide."

Homicides due to asphyxia are not only relatively uncommon, the term itself, "homicidal asphyxia," is rather vague. Depriving a victim of oxygen can be done in a variety of ways. One way, as indicated in Vincent's case, was squeezing the soft tissues of the neck. When his brain had been denied oxygen for a little more than three minutes, Vincent died.

What was not noted in the autopsy report was whether the victim had been raped. Once again, a matter of linkage. If Vincent hadn't been, then it could be the work of another killer. None of it, though, really made any difference. The killer had left nothing behind—no semen, no body fluids, no prints, no fibers. Once again, nothing.

He may have been sloppy in the way he dumped his victims, as Thornton had supposed, but he seemed to be forensically aware. Nobody had seen the black Sonoma truck driven by the portly guy with the mustache and goatee when he dropped off his latest kill on the barbed wire fence in the middle of the night.

The sex with Vincent had been good, but Dominique really got his sexual high from killing. It was something indescribable even to himself, let alone to anyone else. All he knew was that he had to do it. For the police, the disposal of Vincent's body in the open was a tip-off that the killer had changed his MO, a warning that what was to come was the unexpected.

In order to put all the pieces together, a task force would be necessary. Usually commissioned by the state, such a task force would combine local, state, and federal resources into one unit assigned to tracking down the serial killer. But getting the approval from the upper echelons in the state hierarchy to form such a task force had not yet occurred.

Complicating matters, the killings stopped for . . . six months . . . twelve months . . . eighteen months . . . twenty-four months. *For two years,* the serial killer was suddenly inactive. Thornton and the rest of the cops investigating the killings were at a dead end. In itself, that wasn't unusual.

It was the cat-and-mouse game that some serial killers like to play.

CHAPTER FIVE

PIZZA MAN

Louisiana wasn't the only state with a serial killer on the loose. Kansas was having a similar problem with another gentleman who enjoyed killing.

Dennis Rader was leading an anonymous life as a dog-catcher in Park City, a suburb of Wichita, Kansas. He hadn't murdered in more than a decade. After killing ten times, he had stopped. Police were still looking for the self-branded BTK serial killer, while his alter ego, Rader, was doing public service announcements in his dogcatcher role.

Back in Louisiana, Dennis Thornton did not let up, even if the killer had. He kept scanning the reports of Southern Louisiana murders, looking for a lead. Nothing came up. He couldn't figure it out. What had happened? Had the guy moved out of state? There were no BOLOs (Be on the Lookout) from other states that would indicate a killer with the same MO.

In between the demands of his regular caseload, Thornton kept looking. But once again, Ronald J. Dominique hid in plain sight—and simultaneously got in some good eating. Al dente.

Dominique came from Thibodaux, the county seat of Lafourche Parish, halfway between New Orleans and Baton Rouge. He grew up there, in a small town where everyone knew everyone's business. He attended Thibodaux High School, where he was in the glee club and sang in the chorus. Although Dominique was in the closet in school, that didn't stop his classmates from ridiculing him for being gay.

With six siblings, Dominique came from a very large family. As a child, the future serial killer claimed that a priest molested him. His parents didn't believe him, though priest molestation was not an unusual occurrence at the time. As later events would prove, the Catholic Church and local police in many venues from Boston to Los Angeles conspired to protect pedophiliac priests.

Dominique's accusations did nothing to endear him to his parents.

The first time Dominique had a run-in with the police was in June 1985, when he got caught making "dirty phone calls." Arrested and charged with telephone harassment of some of the parish's local residents, he pleaded guilty. He was smart enough to pay a seventy-four-dollar fine plus court costs to avoid jail time.

If someone in law enforcement had been tracking Dominique in the first place, he could have been flagged as someone to watch. Unfortunately, at that time authorities didn't keep tabs on sex offenders. And he behaved himself. Dominique stayed out of trouble with the law for almost nine more years. He next appeared on law enforcement's radar in May 1994. Like too many, he was arrested and charged with drunk driving. Again, nothing suspicious there.

It wasn't until two years later that Dominique's nocturnal activities turned serious.

"He's trying to kill me," a man screamed loudly as he fled from Dominique's bedroom window.

Neighbors heard the scream and immediately called the parish police. Arriving quickly, Lafourche Deputy Sheriff Jimmy McKay arrested Dominique for forcibly raping the partially clad young man and booked him on a $100,000 bond. Dominique couldn't make the bond. So, while the case was winding its way to trial, Dominique spent three months in the county lockup.

Dominique would later claim that during the time he was in custody, prisoners raped him, making his anus particularly susceptible to splitting during sex. That made him determined never to return to jail. Yet if Dominique were convicted of rape, he would serve hard time in Angola, the state's notorious prison for its worst felons.

Finally, Dominique caught a break. The district attorney found himself without a complainant. The young man who claimed that Dominique had raped and almost killed him could not be found. Dominique then had the constitutional right to file a writ of *habeas corpus*.

Habeas corpus is a judicial mandate that orders the prosecution to bring the defendant to court, to determine whether he is being imprisoned unlawfully, without evidence. If there was no complainant, there was no case. In November 1996, the judge continued the case indefinitely, meaning there would be no prosecution.

Ronald J. Dominique was set free, yet his jail time had a profound impact on his life and, eventually, the lives of others. At all costs, he was determined *never* to go back. He vowed that anyone who threatened him with going to the police over anything he did would wind up dead.

From 1997 through New Years Day 2000, Dominique followed through on that vow.

After that, he didn't kill again for two long years. During that time, Thornton wondered what had happened to the serial killer he had been tracking. The answer to Thornton's question was twofold. The first was that Dominique had gotten in trouble with the law, but not for rape and murder. The wannabe Patti LaBelle impersonator had received a summons in May 2000 to appear in a Houma court on charges of disturbing the peace.

What had happened? Well, Dominique had argued forcefully with someone in public, so loud that police were called. Since it was a simple misdemeanor, he was able to plead guilty and pay a fine to avoid even appearing in court. Once again, a court unknowingly offered mercy to the killer. And once again, Dominique still couldn't stay out of trouble.

Almost two years later, on February 10, 2002, the Bayou Blue man was arrested in Houma for allegedly slapping a woman during a Mardi Gras parade. Dominique had accused a woman of hitting a baby stroller in a parking lot with her car. Though the woman apologized, Dominique continued his verbal assault. Finally, the anger boiled to the surface and he couldn't contain it.

It is exceedingly rare in the middle of his killing cycles for a serial killer to keep getting in trouble with the law. If a serial killer has a record, it's usually low-level offenses that take place *prior to the killings*.

And, once again, a police force that had no idea who he really was made a deal. In itself, there was nothing unusual about that. Low-level offenders like Dominique frequently make deals that keep them out of jail. This time, the deal was that instead of standing trial, Dominique was able to enter a parish offenders program.

Such alternative sentencing programs had become common in Louisiana. The idea was to give the offender a second chance while trying to curb future criminal behavior. Alternative sentencing also reduced the number of felons in prison and saved taxpayers their hard-earned wages.

This time, Dominique made the most of the chance that the state gave him. He was a model citizen to the others in the parish program. Meeting all the conditions so he could be discharged and avoid police contact, he came back into society in October 2002. By then, Dominique was busy with his second job.

There isn't a place in the United States that doesn't have at least one Domino's Pizza franchise. Houma had three. If you happened to live in Houma and you ordered a pizza from Domino's, serial killer Ronald J. Dominique was one of the deliverymen who would come to your door.

But Domino's alone couldn't cut it. He still needed more than the pizza money to pay his bills. So Dominique delivered pizzas in the evening while maintaining the day job at the produce company. Work seemed to fill up his time and, for a while, he appeared redeemed. He seemed to enjoy helping people. He was a good employee and tried to be a solid member of the community.

The local Lions Club boasted the dubious distinction of signing up the serial killer as a full member. Dominique spent weekend afternoons calling out the Bingo numbers for senior citizens, because he genuinely liked helping out.

The Lions Club membership director would later recall that he was well liked by everyone there. Maybe Dominique had finally found a place where he felt accepted. But he had other ideas.

"In space, no one can hear you scream."

That was the tagline for the hit Ridley Scott film *Alien* (1979). The line was particularly significant for what Dominique had in mind. Open-area isolation . . . "No one can hear you scream," just like the one sheet for the movie said. Killing in seclusion was just the smart thing to do.

Delivering pizzas all over Houma, Dominique got to see all the young, attractive men. The hustlers, mostly black, working the streets, looking for tricks or drugs or both. Some were gay, some straight; made no difference to him. He just wanted to get them into his car without a struggle.

It required a delicate tongue and maybe some visual stimulation: flashing money. Serial killers like Dominique rely on guile more than force to ensnare their victims. They are con men. But while the hustler thought it was a simple business deal, Dominique was setting him up for something else entirely.

In order to get his prey into a wide, open space where no one would see or hear anything, Dominique went to his brother-in-law Sam Trimble, who unwittingly helped him. Trimble worked at the remote Dixie Shipyard. To get to it, you had to ride three miles over a rutted dirt road that passed through the bayous. It's terrible on the suspension.

Apart from some rusting hulks tied up to the weathered wooden dock in front, the place was desolate. Dominique pulled his trailer over to the middle of a field, where there was nothing around. It was so dark here at night the stars stood out bright in the sky. There wasn't a whisper on the breeze. Such a remote, isolated site would do well.

But there was the problem of body disposal. Pathologists have made a study of how bodies fare in the bayou. They've learned that warm bayou waters accelerate decomposition, making subsequent identification difficult. The longer a body remains in the bayou, the harder it is to identify.

Going inside his trailer, Dominique looked in the mirror. Staring back was a man who was unattractive to himself and to other men. He didn't have sex with men that he didn't buy. What would it be like to have a real relationship? To love someone else who loved him? He was a sociopath. Dominique was not capable of feeling such love.

He may have been good calling the Bingo numbers at the Lion's Club, but nobody wanted to socialize with him, let alone be his friend. It wasn't that he was unfriendly or impolite. People at work identified him for what he was: a loner who kept to himself. By all accounts, Dominique was someone who kept his distance.

In spite of the FBI's involvement and the growing number of murder victims, the story of the Southern Louisiana serial killer failed to be reported nationally. The victims just didn't rate a line of print or a single sound bite.

It wouldn't have made Thornton feel any better to know that the man he was hunting had already killed ten men, tying him with Kansas's now notorious BTK serial killer who was responsible for killing ten and was still at large at the time. BTK killed white, middle-class people. Because of his choice of victims, BTK's activities rated extensive headlines during his three-decade-long killing spree.

The people of Wichita were still on the alert for BTK, but by 2002, in the wake of Al Qaeda's attack on the Twin Towers, the nation had a whole lot of things more important to worry about. America's citizens were on high alert. Where would the terrorists strike next? People were more observant and suspicious. Up in Houma, Louisiana, people were no less paranoid. Little American flags had been attached to every car all over town. No one suspected the real danger in their midst was a serial-killing pizza deliveryman. He wasn't a foreigner. He wasn't a Muslim. And he wasn't a stranger. He was homegrown.

At that very moment, Dominique was restless. He knew— and longed for—the feeling of tying a guy up with his rope, then forcefully pushing his cock into the guy's ass, his cock pulsating, his strong hands tightening around the guy's neck as he struggled. Sometimes, he used a belt or a rope instead.

Of course, he needed to be extra careful of anal sex. The last thing he needed was another operation.

Before he went to prison and was raped, he had been working offshore on one of the oil platforms, back in the early 1990s, and the black pepper he ate went down through his stomach, through his colon and into his rectum. In his ignorance, Dominique believed it was the black pepper that led to his operation and the tight stitch-up. It was actually due to a bacterial infection.

CHAPTER SIX

JOHN DOE

Lafourche and Terrebonne Parishes, October 6, 2002

Kenneth Fitzgerald Randolph Jr. was a Bayou Blue man. He lived near the serial killer, at 146 Charter Court off Bayou Blue Road. He was convenient.

Randolph was five-foot-ten and 150 pounds of muscle. He had close-cropped black hair over a low forehead, deep-set brown eyes, a broad nose, and thick lips that concealed a knowing smile. His twentieth birthday was coming up on August 29, but if he didn't watch it, he might spend it behind bars.

About two years earlier, at age eighteen, Randolph had had his first arrest for "carnal knowledge of a juvenile." Randolph was accused of having consensual sex with a person whose age was, according to official documents, "between thirteen and seventeen." His next arrest was for "criminal damage of property."

In Louisiana, this is a serious felony, punishable by up to fifteen years of hard labor. But Randolph got a minimum sentence, which saw him quickly back on the street. Yet, he just couldn't stay out of trouble. He was arrested a second time for having sex with an underage person. The age is not referred to specifically in official documents to maintain the teen's anonymity.

So far, Randolph had avoided hard jail time through the kinds of compromises common in the criminal justice system. But he liked having sex with kids, a crime the perpetrator usually doesn't stop until he himself is stopped. Five months later, Randolph had sex with a third child.

This time, he was handed a felony conviction, and yet Randolph was given a gift: a very light sentence of three years in prison, sentence suspended, with eighteen months of supervised probation.

Back on the street, Randolph the pedophile met Dominique the serial killer.

Cane fields are common to Southern Louisiana, where the warm climate nurtures the fibrous plant. It is one of the state's best crops; fields stretch for miles. Finding them is no surprise, but discovering the naked body of a young black man lying in one is definitely uncommon. The corpse had been dumped, face down, in a cane field in Lafourche Parish, in a very rural area near a pumping station.

The police cordoned off the area while the criminalists scoured the field around the body for evidence. Approaching the body a short time later, Lafourche Parish Sheriff's Office detective Tom Atkins noted that the victim was completely naked, except for the socks. He was still wearing white Champion-brand socks.

Detective Atkins looked at the body's position. It was sprawled arms forward and down, legs stretched out. It didn't look like Randolph had been there too long, but the heat and humidity had accelerated decomposition of the body. That made getting the corpse to the medical examiner all the more imperative. They didn't want any more decomposition that could destroy evidence of homicide.

Wearing surgical gloves, Atkins picked up and examined the guy's wrists, which revealed ligature marks. The throat showed the same kind of ligature marks. At first glance, it looked like the victim had been bound and strangled. Also, the killer had positioned the body so that his buttocks stuck out.

In addition to indicating MO, body position is a fact known only by the perpetrator and the investigative team on the scene. It is knowledge the detective can later use to his or her advantage during the questioning of a suspect. Since only the killer would know such an intimate detail, admitting it during questioning could help seal a first-degree murder conviction and put him in the death chamber. That is, as long as the court admitted as evidence the killer's statement to the cops.

Atkins made sure that the photographer on the scene got a close-up of the guy's rectum. He also made sure to ask the criminalists to print the guy before bagging him. Soon after returning to his office, Atkins had the results of the fingerprint check.

Atkins contacted Randolph's family with the sad news of his death. Now it was time for the coroner to do his thing. Since his election fourteen years earlier, Dr. Robert Treuting had been the Jefferson County coroner. Treuting was a very popular official.

Some states don't require the coroner to be a medical doctor. Louisiana isn't one of them. By Louisiana state law, the coroner must be a medical doctor. Indeed, the multitalented Treuting helped to design and build Jefferson Parish Forensic Center in Harvey, Louisiana, one of the most advanced forensic facilities in the country. As a member of the Jefferson Parish Community Justice Agency, the coroner and his staff are charged with death and sexual-assault investigations.

By the time the corpse of Kenneth Randolph was placed on the forensic pathologist's table, his toe tag had changed. He had been the anonymous "John Doe" when found. Upon his fingerprint identification, that was changed to "Kenneth Randolph," giving him back his humanity. The date was October 6, 2002.

The next morning at 9:50 a.m., forensic pathologist Brittany Somers began the autopsy. Detective Tom Atkins was present to lend a hand and gather evidence. The coroner collected oral and anal swabs and smears, pubic hair, head hair, right and left fingernail scrapings and clippings, and a purple tube of blood.

Dr. Somers also collected hair from the left sock and parts of the body. Material like this that was gathered for the sexual assault kit could later be matched with the DNA of a suspect, providing the kind of direct evidence that would lead to a conviction. That is, unless the accused could afford a high-priced attorney who knew how to challenge the evidence.

Randolph was cold to the touch. He had not made it the few weeks to his twentieth birthday. His corpse was well preserved, still in the middle stages of rigor mortis, which revealed that Randolph had been dead for only four or five hours, the time it takes for rigor mortis to fully set into a body.

Somers looked at Randolph's head for signs of injury, including lacerations or bludgeoning. Nothing appeared abnormal as she examined his close-cropped, coarse, curly, dark-brown hair. But there was a long, horizontal linear abrasion on his forehead, extending down his neck and to his chest.

Somers pulled the dead man's eyelids up and looked in his eyes, where she observed "conjunctival congestion with petechiae and confluence hemorrhages." Strangulation. There were numerous small abrasions around his thighs and a linear red contusion on the right buttock. On the wrists, the pathologist saw a large contusion surrounding the right one and a smaller one on the left.

It looked like Randolph's wrists had been tied up with something, the right wrist tighter than the left, which accounted for the wrist's hemorrhage. The body abrasions might indicate that the killer forced Randolph down onto his chest and forehead, so he could have easy access to his anus. That would account for the numerous scrapes on his thighs and the cut on the right buttock.

The coroner's lawful duty is to determine the cause of death. Picking up her scalpel, Somers cut into the neck and confirmed a "hemorrhage on the underlying soft tissue" surrounding the hyoid bone. The bone itself was intact, but there was a hemorrhage farther down the throat on the epiglottis, beneath the vocal cords of the larynx.

Everything else was normal; nothing unusual in the body cavities and organs. Somers wrote in her summary, "It is my opinion that Kenneth Randolph Jr. died as a result of strangulation. While a ligature mark was obvious, a component of manual strangulation cannot be excluded. The manner of death is homicide."

That meant that for whatever reason, the killer had not only choked Randolph with some sort of rope, he had also choked him with his hands. It was unclear which came first, though an educated guess might be that if the rope didn't do the job, the killer resorted to his hands. The autopsy had also proven that Randolph had been raped before death.

The contents of the sexual assault kit and Randolph's clothing were turned over to Detective Atkins for tests.

Dominique's kill total was now up to eleven. He walked up to a house in Houma and rang the doorbell.

"You called for a pizza?" he said brightly to the man who answered the door.

CHAPTER SEVEN

BIG JULIUS AND NOKA JONES

Houma and Lafourche Parishes, October 12–15, 2002

Dominique had been living in Terrebonne Parish for almost three years. It was a backwater place that would become infamous as the home base of the new millennium's most horrific serial killings.

In town at a shabby apartment complex on Fremont Street, Shelly Weston was waiting in Apartment B for her boyfriend to come back inside after smoking his cigarette. She called him "Noka" for short. His full name was Anoka T. Jones. Small and muscular at five-foot-seven and 137 pounds, Noka was an affectionate man.

Like many born into poverty, crime followed Noka—or he followed crime. His first conviction, in 1996, was for conspiracy to distribute illegal drugs. He followed that up a year later with convictions for simple theft and battery. In 1997, he was arrested again for the same offenses and was convicted once more.

Noka dodged one court warrant after another. Noka, though, loved Shelly Weston. Maybe that would make a difference in the long run.

When she got off work on Saturday afternoon, October 12, Weston went grocery shopping. Coming home between 7:00 and 7:30 p.m., Noka helped her put the groceries away. Then around eight, Noka left on his bicycle to get a pack of cigarettes.

Trolling for his next victim, Ronald J. Dominique was driving in the area.

As the Sonoma drifted down the street, Dominique spied a slim young black man on a bicycle just up ahead. The guy hadn't seen him yet. He had to make sure not to frighten him, lest he bolt or refuse the offer. Dominique expertly turned the wheel of the Sonoma to the right, coming up parallel to the guy on the bike.

As his foot eased up on the gas pedal to match the cyclist's slower pace, he reached over and rolled down the passenger-side window.

"Hey, can we talk?" Dominique asked smoothly.

Noka looked inside and saw nothing dangerous about the pudgy white guy. Hitting his brakes, he pulled his bike over to the curb. Straddling the seat of his bike, Noka and the guy began to chat through the open window of the Sonoma. Soon they had finished their conversation and Noka began riding again.

He rode at a fast clip up the block and back to his house. He had money on his mind. That always motivated him. As he came in the front door, his girlfriend noticed that Noka already had a cigarette, like he was ready to light up.

"Where you going?" she asked.

"I'm just going to stand outside and smoke a cigarette," Noka said.

"Okay," she replied. "No harm in that."

First, though, Noka brought his bicycle inside the house. He relied on the bike for transportation, as did many of Houma's poorer residents. Like every night, Noka hugged and kissed Weston.

"I love you," he said quietly.

Then he was out the door. Weston didn't worry about it when she went to sleep and Noka wasn't there. "Going out for a smoke" wasn't to be taken literally. What it really meant was that sometimes he wasn't back until late. He had things to do.

Noka Jones didn't have to worry about the long-term effects of smoke on the lungs of his twenty-six-year-old body. He was in the fatal back seat of Dominique's black Sonoma.

It was about ten o'clock and the highway was crowded with cars going up to the Big Easy for the night. The other side of the highway was also crowded, because everyone knew that Houma had better Cajun and Creole cooking than New Orleans, and at half the price, no less. Or, you could just drift into one of the bars where, for less than ten bucks, you got a full plate of shrimp fresh from the Gulf, with mayonnaise and ketchup to make your own remoulade sauce.

Dominique didn't know whose body was in the back seat. He couldn't remember the guy's name, or even if he'd said his name. *Who cared?* Covered by a blanket, Dominique had the right idea—to get rid of it. Last thing he needed was for a cop to stop him with a body in the back. He had left Houma for Lafourche. Some miles farther on, he was almost in his home parish.

He got on Interstate 310 toward New Orleans and drove down the now-familiar ramp, passing the black-and-white Jefferson County Sheriff's Office squad car parked at the foot waiting for speeders. Inside the Sonoma, Dominique's groin was throbbing. The thrill of having the body in the back seat and driving past the cop who was unaware of what had happened was just tremendous.

If he could have slowed down to make the thrill last longer, he would have, but to do that would be to invite attention. He kept going, made a left, and disappeared from view.

The next morning, Officer John Smith was on active patrol in the Boutte area. At about 10:30 a.m., he happened to see out the window of his squad car a black man wearing a blue shirt and black shorts, lying motionless. Smith was on a dirt road under the Interstate 310 overpass, on the northbound side. The officer parked and walked slowly toward the victim.

Looking down at him, still not touching anything, Smith saw dried blood around the victim's mouth. He was lying forward on his stomach and Smith could also see a small laceration on his lower back. Smith bent down and took his wrist pulse; nothing. He tried the jugular vein; still nothing. No surprise there. The body was rigid; rigor mortis had set in.

Smith saw drag marks on the dirt road. They appeared to have been made by the victim's hands, after being dragged in an eastward direction. He saw that the victim's shirt was raised midway up his chest, while his shorts were down to the mid-thigh area.

Smith was a patrol officer, not a manhunter. His job was to take the initial observations and then bring in the pros. It was time to turn it over to the detectives and criminalists. Smith called it in, advised the parish detective bureau and the patrol supervisor of what he'd found, then moved to secure the crime scene. Quickly, he set up the yellow crime-scene tape that would keep unwanted eyes away from a full murder investigation.

Answering Smith's summons was Detective James DeFelice. DeFelice observed not only the drag marks made from the victim's hands but also tire impressions that would be consistent with a car. DeFelice deduced that the killer drove in, pulled the body out of the car by the feet so the hands dragged in the dirt, and then dumped it and drove away.

The killer did nothing to disguise the body or the dump site.

Criminalists arrived and used latent-fingerprint-lifting tape on the legs, arms, and right hand of the deceased in an attempt to collect any small trace of fiber or hair that might be present and could later be matched to the perpetrator. Detective DeFelice, meanwhile, had no idea he and Dennis Thornton had something in common: they were searching for the same killer.

DeFelice hadn't seen the sketch of the Louisiana serial killer, knew nothing about him, and had no reason to attribute this homicide to anyone other than a run-of-the-mill murderer. The first thing to do was figure out who the victim was. A search of his pockets turned up nothing. DeFelice left the scene to the criminalists, marking off bits of evidence with their red cones.

Soon, the morgue attendants came and performed their routine tasks. The "John Doe" was wrapped in a clean white sheet, placed into a standard polyurethane body bag, and zipped up for transport to the county morgue. Back at headquarters, DeFelice ran the victim's prints through the FBI and state computer database in an attempt to identify the victim.

Up came the match: "Anoka T. Jones," along with his criminal record. Now they had a name they could put to the John Doe on the coroner's table. A good autopsy answers all the questions about how a victim dies. Its success, or failure, is dependent on the person performing the autopsy, and more importantly, on their considered observations.

On October 14 at promptly 7:00 a.m., Tyler Bodie, the parish coroner, looked down at the body of Anoka Jones. He noticed the neck abrasions. Writing a short time later in his

summary of the cause of death, Dr. Bodie said: "With the his-
torical and investigation information presently available, cause
of death as determined by autopsy and toxicological analysis
is considered to be asphyxia by strangulation (neck ligature).
Manner of death is considered to be homicide."

Detectives went over to Noka's home, where they found
his girlfriend still anxiously awaiting his return. They showed
Somers a photograph of Noka's face taken before the autopsy.
Identifying it, she gave the cops the basic information about the
bike and the cigarette, then broke down sobbing when they told
her of the discovery.

Leaving Noka's girlfriend to her grief, the police next focused
their attention on one of Noka's friends, Leon Lirette. At the
shabby house he shared with his mother, Lirette told them that
the last time he'd seen Noka was on the evening of October 13
at about 9:00 p.m.

"I had asked Noka to come over and help me move some
speakers," Lirette told detectives. "He did, and after we finished,
he asked to use the phone. My mother let him. He spoke for a
second, then hung up."

"I'll see you later T-Paul," he had said, using Lirette's nickname, and walked out the door.

Back in Houma, where Noka Jones had lived, the Terrebonne Parish detective squad had already sent out detectives
to investigate potential criminal activity Jones might have been
involved in. They came back with the information that Noka
sold drugs for two local dealers, Josh Beymer and Barry Green-
berg. He also owed them money, which could certainly be a
motive to murder him, but not to rape him.

They soon found a friend, Belle Grammand, who spoke to
Noka shortly before his murder. He called her on the phone
at about 10:30 p.m. to tell her that he had some "shake" (crack

cocaine crumbs) and to ask if she wanted to smoke some with him. She told him she no longer smoked and hung up the phone. Further investigation brought forth a "possible witness" by the name of Ron Gibbons.

Gibbons told detectives that he was at the corner of Naquin Street and Hobson Street with Noka when a gray truck with its lights off approached them. When the truck stopped, two guys came out and confronted Noka, who took off running. In the back seat was "Big Julius"; Gibbons didn't know his real name.

Continued digging turned up the name of one of Noka's known drug associates, Julius Bellows, a.k.a. Big Julius. Figuring he could be the prime suspect, the deputies seized Bellows's car and began a search for trace blood evidence while detectives spoke with him. Big Julius claimed Noka used to come over to his house all the time to buy crack. But he denied any involvement in his former customer's death. "If anyone says I did it," he told detectives, "he's a liar! I will give you hair samples, shoe samples, or anything if you want to clear me of any involvement."

Because he was cooperative, the cops believed him. Bellows was released from custody. Besides, still another suspect had emerged. He was Jesus Gonder, a.k.a. "Tricky." Hailing from Houston, he was a twenty-seven-year-old black man with a record of small-time drug felonies. He also was pretty good at hiding out; they couldn't find Tricky.

Lafourche detectives pored over their interview reports and other evidence in their case files. At the same time, their counterparts in Jefferson were doing exactly the same thing on the body-dump job in their venue—that of Kenny Randolph.

Thornton doesn't remember who it was that first saw the similarities in the homicides and reached out, but he soon found himself in a room with detectives from Lafourche Parish, comparing notes on the murders of Anoka Jones and Kenny Randolph. Thornton saw the similarities. He figured, correctly, that the guy who killed Noka Jones was the serial killer he was hunting. Interviews were set up with friends and close relatives of both decedents to see if they had any common enemies.

Once again, Somers told police her story, adding nothing new. She knew none of the people involved in the Randolph case. Others were reinterviewed too; no links. For Dennis Thornton, it wasn't so much disappointing as it was disheartening. Thornton had a street cop's common sense. The detective from Jefferson Parish knew it was no accident the victims didn't rate a line of print or one soundbite. They weren't considered valuable enough, by anyone, to be a priority one way or the other. There was therefore no internal pressure to bring the killer to justice. To Dennis Thornton, that made no difference. He couldn't, *wouldn't* let it go, which was just as well.

Back in Terrebonne Parish, Dominique hooked his trailer up to his Sonoma and prepared to tow it out of the shipyard. The Bayou Blue man was on the move.

Time to troll.

PART TWO

THE INVESTIGATION

CHAPTER EIGHT

GRANDPA SOCKS

Terrebonne Parish, Saturday, May 24, 2003

Datrell Woods was a real piece of work.

Released from jail a few months earlier, the teenager was hanging out on a sunny spring afternoon at his house, which he shared with his mother and sister, on Buron Street in Houma

About three o'clock, Datrell changed clothes in his bedroom, then relaxed for the next three hours. At six, Datrell was talking to his cousin Frank Wilson, who was visiting.

"I'm going stay at my girlfriend's house in Mott Trailer Park," Datrell informed his cousin.

Wilson had something a little bit more important on his mind.

"Look—my mom got a call from a man who said he was going to kill everyone in the house if he did not get his rings back," said Wilson.

It seemed that Datrell was engaged in a little habit of breaking and entering. Or, put another way, he was a burglar who preferred the same victim. Datrell had been continually breaking into this dude's house at the corner of Elder Street and stealing stuff. He claimed the guy had given him permission to take some of his things as payment for a debt. Datrell also tried to sell the Brooklyn Bridge for five dollars to anyone who was interested.

Datrell went back over to the dude's house. When he emerged a short while later, his friend Gary Birdwright was waiting for him. They had served time in prison together. A car pulled up to the curb, a Toyota Celica, with a few other people in it. Gary opened the door. Datrell was ready to dive in when the words made him freeze.

"Datrell, would you get me a glass of water," his mother, Margaret Woods, called from the ramshackle house.

Like a good son, Datrell reversed direction and went back in the house. After getting his mother the water, Datrell came out of the house a second time. He was wearing a white polo shirt that hung longer in the rear than the front, with light-green stripes near the buttons. He had on the brown socks he'd gotten as a present from an aunt, which Datrell called his "grandpa socks." Over them, he sported black three-quarter-top Nikes with the silver swoosh.

Datrell got into the Celica and it drove off. Interviewed later, Datrell's mother, Margaret, remembered things a little differently.

Datrell had been walking on Buron Street with "a white guy named Gary when another white guy who was sitting on the driver's side and the white girl who was sitting on the passenger side passed my house in a white car. It had black stripes."

They turned off Leona Street, back onto Buron. That's when she called her son back to get her the water. Maybe it was a premonition or perhaps that elusive bond between mother and son. Whatever it was, Margaret Woods felt something was wrong. The "water story" was just that—a pretext to get her baby boy back in the house, where he was safe and sound.

"Datrell, don't leave," she pleaded with her son, once he was safely inside.

Datrell thought a moment.

"I'm going to stay by my friend's house," he reassured his mother reasonably.

She knew that Datrell hung with Gary. But she reminded him that he had an appointment down at Social Security on May 27. Datrell ignored the remark. He could take care of social security any time. Besides, Datrell had left his bike at Gary's house. It was his major means of transportation and he needed it. Datrell got his mother the water and left her house.

His mother watched him get into the Toyota Celica with Gary, and the car drove off into a dark abyss.

It was a nice, cool morning, and Corey Hood, twenty-one years old, felt like riding his three-wheeler. So he got together with his cousin Joshua Robicheaux, a twenty-three-year-old dirt-bike enthusiast, to go out dirt biking together.

"I was riding my dirt bike in the field off of Highway 56 near Woodlawn Ranch Road. My cousin Corey Hood was riding his three-wheeler. While we was riding, Corey's chain came off. We was headed toward Woodlawn Ranch Road. I took a left on the dirt road and saw something lying in the road. When I saw it, it looked like a body," said Robicheaux.

Robicheaux rode closer, to see if he was right. He stopped and saw that it was, indeed, a body. It looked like it had been there for a while, because the corpse was "puffy." There was also a bicycle lying a couple of feet away from his head.

Robicheaux turned the wheels of his dirt bike around and rode back to where Corey was still stuck

"It looks like someone's laying in the dirt road!" Robicheaux shouted.

Corey finished fixing his chain and hopped on the seat. They rode back purposefully, to view the corpse together. It was now covered with flies. To a pathologist, that would indicate the body had been there for some time and decomposition was well along. Corey figured, correctly, "that there was nothing they could do for him but call the police."

Getting back on the bikes, they rode quickly to a nearby casino, where they hailed an employee who was dumping trash outside.

"Call the police because we saw a body!" Robicheaux announced to the surprised worker.

"We found a body in the cane field," Corey added.

The worker ran for a phone and dialed 911. A few minutes later, two police officers arrived. Pulling up in their marked units, they asked the cousins to show them where the body was. The boys told the police the location and they headed that way. The cousins got back on their bikes and rode after them, to view what would now be considered a crime scene, and later, a dump site.

The second time viewing the body, Corey took in more detail. He noted that the black man wore blue jean shorts and brown socks. Curiously, he wasn't wearing a shirt.

Detective Simon Fryman of the Houma City Police Department was at home when he got the call from dispatch. When Fryman arrived at the location, he was met by uniformed officers and briefed on the situation. They took the detective over to speak with Robicheaux and Hood, who told him of their grisly discovery.

They had found a black man who was dead and puffy. Fryman thought about that for a moment, taking note of the weather. It was partly cloudy and about eighty-five degrees. It had been several days since it had rained. The ground in the area was very dry and arid. On closer inspection, Fryman noticed that there was no dirt on the bottom of the victim's socks. That implied that he was dumped, rather than dragged, to the location.

The detective saw that lying just south of the body was a bicycle, a red beach cruiser. Fryman noticed the clean treads; there was no dirt on the tires. Nor were there tire tracks to indicate that the bike had been ridden into the area, but there were impressions made in the dirt by the handlebar and the pedal.

It appeared someone had physically thrown the bike down.

The detective noted that the victim's face was quite swollen and that large blisters were forming on the body. Fryman looked at the eyes, but because of the decomposition, he was unable to detect any petechial hemorrhaging. He also spotted a tattoo on the right arm: the letters "VW."

As if things weren't strange enough, there was more: a fluid-like substance around the body. Yet the detective couldn't identify any injuries from which the fluid might have seeped. Nor was there any identification on the body. The guy had really been stripped.

Once criminalists arrived on the scene, Fryman rolled the victim onto his side and checked for any possible injuries. None were visible. Preservation was all-important. The body was bagged and taken away. Due to the state of decomposition and the stink of the body as it decayed, it was immediately shoved into the freezer at the morgue. The cold would stop both.

They'd keep him on ice for a while and then the detectives could come in and fingerprint the victim to get his identification. A few hours later, the body was removed from the cooler to be fingerprinted by investigator Donald McCord. Fryman and his investigative team then went to the Terrebonne Parish Sheriff's Office Crime Lab, where he requested a fingerprint comparison be done using the Automated Fingerprint Identification System (AFIS) database. The results were phoned to him that evening.

"We've got a confirmation on the fingerprints," said the excited voice of Detective Frank Foran over the phone.

Foran explained that a sergeant with the Terrebonne Parish Sheriff's Office Crime Scene Unit had called him earlier with a match to a subject named Datrell Woods. It may have been a big parish but it was a small town. On a case in the past, Fryman had encountered the Woods family.

Fryman knew Datrell Woods's mother, Margaret, and that the Woods family resided on Elder Street. He remembered that the last time he spoke to her, the family was in the process of moving. Fryman didn't know if they had indeed moved out or not, but Elder Street seemed like a good place to start the field investigation.

When Fryman and the detectives arrived at the Elder Street address, the first thing they noticed was there were no curtains hanging at the windows. Looking inside, they didn't see any furniture. The place was clearly unoccupied. Fryman knew of a Woods relative, Ellen Finch, on Main Street. They drove over to question her but she wasn't home.

Fryman recalled that Finch was employed at the McDonald's located near the intersection of Grand Caillou Road and Industrial Boulevard. They found Ellen's husband, Cyrus, sitting there in the parking lot.

"Do you know where I can find Margaret Woods?" Fryman asked.

"Check with my wife inside," Cyrus said, gesturing to the hamburger joint.

Ellen Finch was working the takeout window. Fryman flashed his badge and asked where Margaret Woods lived. Finch gave him an address on Buron Street. When they got there, Fryman asked the man who opened the door if he could speak to Margaret Woods. A few minutes later, she appeared and Fryman walked her outside to his car.

"When was the last time you saw your son, Datrell?" he asked softly.

"Yesterday," said Margaret.

"No, it could not have been yesterday," Fryman replied, bearing in mind the condition of the body.

Margaret thought again.

"It was during the weekend," she answered. "I talked to him about an appointment he has with the Social Security Department."

They chatted a bit longer about a few of the details of the last time she saw her son. As Fryman listened, he knew it was leading to the inevitable.

"Detectives recovered the remains of an individual in a cane field off Woodlawn Road near Highway 56 that was identified as Datrell."

Margaret listened, shocked at the details of the discovery. She started sobbing and ran inside to tell her family the dreadful news. Family members came outside and began shouting questions at the detective. But Fryman had a question of his own. He allowed family members to look at the bike that they had recovered near the body.

"Was this Datrell's?" he asked.

Sure enough, it was identified as Datrell's bicycle. Everywhere he went, Datrell rode that exact bicycle. He was never far from it.

On May 28, Dr. Susan Garcia performed the autopsy on Datrell Woods at the state-of-the-art Jefferson Parish Forensics Center.

The preliminary results showed no signs of trauma to the body. There were no signs of Woods having been shot or stabbed. Blunt force trauma was ruled out as well; there were no wounds, defensive or otherwise. There were also no signs that the feet or hands of their victim had been bound. But the body had been preserved long enough to note that cause of death was asphyxiation. He'd been strangled.

Although toxicology results would take a few days, they had the cause of death and didn't expect anything unusual to be revealed in the report. The family did tell the police about Datrell's friend Gary. Was he a suspect? Fryman and some other detectives rode on horseback to the dump site for a more intensive search.

Slowly, the horses were directed around the area. The detectives eyed everything for evidence or clues. Unfortunately, their search was fruitless.

Once back at the station, a detective handed Fryman Datrell Woods's record. Fryman wasn't surprised to learn that Woods had been locked up in the juvenile jail system, starting in 1996. Put into custody at Bridge City, a group home, he left in 2000. But soon he was in trouble again. Woods was sent to Jetson Correctional Center and then Swanson Correctional Center in Tallulah.

In reading the records, Fryman noticed that Woods had been cared for by social worker Jeannette Dupree. He called her office—she wasn't in and he left a message with the receptionist for her to call back. Then he got a phone call from a "good Samaritan." A man named Jonathan Burdick said that about 12:30 to 1:00 p.m. on Sunday, he was passing the area near where the body had been found, when he saw a white or cream-colored car parked on the dirt road in the cane field.

That appeared suspicious to him. Burdick wasn't sure exactly what kind of car it was or if anybody was in it. But as he looked back, it appeared that the car was moving. Once Burdick turned onto Louisiana Highway 56, he couldn't see it anymore.

No sooner had Fryman hung up the phone than it rang again. Jeannette Dupree was returning his call. Dupree told Fryman that Woods had been in correctional centers for two years. She said the only other person she knew from Houma who had been locked up with Woods was James Jefferson. Jefferson and Woods got along. She added some sad details.

"Datrell's family was not supportive of him at all. They were barely in touch with Datrell while he was in lockdown."

"How about visitors?"

"The family had virtually no contact. They wouldn't even supply him with basic necessities, like underclothes. He said his mom never called. Oh, and Datrell was slow in his learning capabilities."

By early afternoon, Fryman had found Woods's brother, Willie Woods, at the family home on Buron Street. They brought him in for questioning. Willie recalled his last meeting with his brother vividly. He'd seen Datrell on Saturday evening, about 6:00 p.m.

Then he added, "Before you picked me up, my mom got a call from a man who said he was going to kill everyone in the house if he did not get his rings back."

It seemed that Datrell had stolen the guy's rings.

Fryman returned to the Royal Flush Casino, where the cousins had found the worker who made the 911 call. He asked Sam Blaine, the head of security for the casino, to check his surveillance cameras for anything suspicious. He gave him CDs to burn in case he found information that he could copy and pass on to the detectives.

Now it was time to get to Gary. The Woods family had identified him as Gary Stevens. They drove out to Robert Street where Stevens lived with his mother. He wasn't home, but his mother was.

"Gary's somewhere in Bayou Blue and hasn't been home recently," she said.

Fryman also spoke to Gary's brother, Jonathan, who said that neither he nor Gary hung out with Woods.

"People been saying that we hang together, but neither of us hung with Datrell," he told Fryman.

A few days later, Fryman received a phone call that Stevens had been located. He was back home. Fryman immediately picked Stevens up and took him to the Houma Police Department headquarters for an interview. He was very cooperative.

"Last time I saw Datrell was about a month ago," said Stevens. "I was never locked up with Datrell. The only time I was locked up was approximately three years ago for a burglary."

The detectives were curious if he had a girlfriend.

"I don't have a girlfriend, haven't had one for about a year. I really don't think I'm the 'Gary' Datrell's family talked about. The only friends I hang out with are P-Dot and John, and I don't know their names. And I stay on Jerome Court, on the east side of Houma."

"Do you know Willie Woods?" Fryman asked.

"I'm familiar with Willie. I hung out with him or knew him from school, but I never hung out with Datrell and I was never at Datrell's house."

Based on the interview, Gary Stevens did not appear to be the subject the family was referring to who was hanging around with Datrell. But one thing was for sure—Datrell Woods wasn't going to make his Social Security appointment anytime soon.

Through his research, Fryman eventually became aware of the previous killings. He made the linkage to the serial killer working Southern Louisiana. Dennis Thornton was contacted. Looking at the Datrell Woods case file, Thornton knew immediately the suspect was the serial killer he'd been tracking through the end of the last millennium.

A few articles about the murders had appeared in local papers and didn't go national. Thornton knew a lack of resources was preventing the police from solving the case. He knew what was needed: a full-fledged task force, dedicated to tracking the murderer down. That way they could *pool all* their resources.

But to upper-level authorities, the murderer who had killed Datrell Woods and the others was just one guy. And the victims, well, no one really wanted to talk about what the killer had done to them. There were many other murderers, drug dealers, and thieves working the parishes who also needed to be caught. And maybe some of those victims were taxpayers, unlike the hustlers who were the serial killer's victims.

Thornton recalls of the case, "The attitude was don't break your neck."

CHAPTER NINE

THE METER READER

Terrebonne Parish, 2006

Things changed for Dominique in January 2004. That's when Caro Produce laid him off.

Being the diligent worker he was, he soon got a job with Gulf Coast Maintenance in Houma, staying six months until he quit. Then Dominique got the perfect job for someone keeping a low profile. He became a meter reader.

Let's face it: that's the *perfect* job for a serial killer.

Dominique was employed by a meter-reading company through the end of 2004. During that entire time—in fact, since the first of the year—Dominique didn't murder anyone. Dominique was smarter than most serial killers, having remained undetected for so long, and with so many victims. He had found that killing in Houma was very different from killing in New Orleans and its suburbs.

While New Orleans had a series of highways and streets

around each dump site, which always made for a swift getaway, Houma was a rural town. It can be risky to dump a body in a rural town; if he didn't know the roads, he could easily get lost. But in Houma he was getting to know the roads—and learning which ones to take to find a little privacy.

He wouldn't, however, go the extra mile into the bayou. Supposing once he'd finished dumping somebody, he got lost on the way back? That would make him a target for the police. That's the last thing he wanted. So far, no one he knew had been questioned about the murders. While he obviously never spoke about it, Dominique must have known he was being hunted. After all, he had deliberately dropped the bodies in ways that would attract the cops.

Every day on the way to work, he passed by the Terrebonne Parish Sheriff's Office. He knew what he was doing. He never once attracted the attention of them or the cops in any of the other parishes. If he didn't know for sure that the police were on his tail, he sure acted like he did.

Dominique used the time on the clock to plan future killings. If it were later proven in court that he was planning first-degree murder, he'd have a quick march to the death chamber regardless of who was on the Supreme Court.

His meter-reading job took Dominique all through Terrebonne Parish, into the outlying areas. Dominique found himself on more than one occasion driving his truck up a dirt road in the middle of nowhere, just to read someone's meter. He became familiar with the roads and he began to make mental notes for future body-dump sites.

One place stood out. It was on a backwater road, a Shriners meeting hall. Behind it, near the local airport, was a dense patch of woods and a field.

During the years that Dominique abstained from killing, police made no progress in tracking him down.

They knew there were thirteen murders in five different parishes, all linked by MO. It was the same in every case—strangulation. Cops referred to them as "soft kills." There were no motives that could be associated with any of the victims' families, friends, or even enemies. That, of course, is consistent with serial killing. Nor did police have a viable suspect.

Thornton, Fryman, and every other detective working the case had sat down in front of computer screens in their offices. Thornton himself had been through every database he had access to, of men charged and/or convicted of sex offenses, and still had no viable leads. It was more than frustrating; it was dispiriting. Sometimes he found his broad shoulders sagging under the weight.

They might have sagged further had he known that Dominique was indeed in another parish's database. Having been charged with male-on-male rape many years before, the serial killer's identity was waiting to be discovered by a keen-eyed detective. Absent that, police could always hold out the hope that someplace down the line, they might match some left-behind DNA to their "not yet" suspect.

Dennis Thornton knew it was necessary to establish a special task force. With a dedicated group of officers pooling their information, resources, and intelligence, they'd have a better shot at identifying and catching the killer.

One night, Dominique found himself driving out in the parish with a tropical storm raging all around him. This was Tropical Storm Matthew, which ravaged Southern Louisiana in October 2004. Eighty-mile-an-hour winds lashed at roofs as rain pounded down in sheets for a full day. At times, the rain was horizontal because of the intense winds, and the temperature fell as the storm reached its peak. It finally ended during the night. The next morning dawned sunny and bright.

Banker Jeff Murrow was the first to notice the body lying near a pond in the Des Allemands area. Murrow drove home. He knocked on the door of his neighbor Don Jerome. By pure coincidence, Jerome was a criminalist with the sheriff's office of St. Charles Parish. He responded immediately to his neighbor's summons.

Racing to his car, Jerome drove toward the location that Murrow had described. He got there in twenty minutes. At 11:40 a.m., Jerome located the body of a "black male," as he later detailed in his report. Jerome notified dispatch and went back to his observations. The victim lay on his right side, knees slightly bent; no visible signs of trauma; and rigor mortis not yet present.

Jerome went through the pockets of the victim's blue sweat pants and black polo-style short-sleeved shirt. The criminalist could find no identification. No socks, no shoes. And he was very wet. The killer had dumped the body while the tropical storm still raged.

It was a desperate thing to do, going out in weather like that, when a flying tree could kill you instantly. But if you happen to have killed somebody and you have already transferred them to your car, dumping the body is of the highest priority, lest you be discovered. Dominique did not dally after a kill. He immediately disposed of his victims.

Jerome searched the area for trace evidence and found nothing. A few minutes later, he took digital photographs of the deceased and the surrounding recovery area. Then detectives arrived on the scene. A rough sketch and measurements were taken of the dump site. Shortly after, the coroner's investigator arrived to officially pronounce the victim dead and have the body removed to the morgue.

The autopsy took place the following day, with Jerome in attendance at the "post mortem examination of an unidentified black male subject (John Doe)." Jerome took digital photographs of the victim prior to and during the autopsy, conducted by Dr. Frank Johnson. Johnson eventually concluded that whoever had killed the victim had used *a lot* of force.

Johnson's official autopsy report says that he found blunt force trauma to the right shoulder and soft tissue and intramuscular hemorrhages of the back and buttocks. For some reason, that was not found to be unusual. Instead, Johnson wrote: "Signs of violence are not apparent at the scene. Cause of death as determined at autopsy and toxicological analysis is considered to be drug overdose (cocaine). Manner of death is considered to be accidental."

It probably wasn't the first time, or the last, that a victim of a serial killer was listed first as an "accidental" death, in this case from a cocaine overdose. That did, of course, contradict the autopsy finding where Johnson found "lineal abrasions of each buttock . . . vascular hemorrhage within the subcutaneous fatty tissues."

Could the victim have been raped? The coroner didn't comment. As for method of death, a neck dissection "noted overlying the strap muscles of the anterior right neck . . . is red-currant jelly-clotted blood." That would be consistent with strangulation. After the autopsy was completed, the victim's prints were gathered and entered in the AFIS.

A short time later, the prints came back identifying the victim as "Larry Matthews of Thibodaux." They also got his last known address. Turned out detectives from the Thibodaux Police Department were already familiar with Larry Matthews. A known drug dealer and user, he was described in police reports as "somewhat homeless."

How exactly someone could be "somewhat homeless" was not quite explained.

The Thibodaux cops had met Matthews's brother, Martin, during a prior investigation of Matthews's drug dealing. When they went to his residence to interview him, Martin said that he had last seen his brother three or four days ago and was worried about him. He remembered seeing him walking south on Charles Street and then disappearing in the distance.

The cops told Martin that his brother had been found dead. They had positively identified Larry Matthews through his fingerprints.

"Do you know anyone who would want your brother dead?" a detective asked.

"I can't think of anyone my brother hung around with or anyone wanting to do him harm."

Four days later—well past the seventy-two-hour window of opportunity in a murder investigation (most successful cases are solved in that time frame)—the phone rang at the Thibodaux Parish Sheriff's Office.

"This is Simon Fryman of the Houma Police Department," said the voice on the line.

Fryman told Thibodaux police that they had a "white male" at their office, Jim Jarmin, claiming that the police were looking for him. It was in reference to Larry Matthews's murder.

"Jarmin said that he was visiting a friend in Thibodaux when Larry Matthews showed up. He lent his wife's vehicle to Matthews and he has not got it back yet," Fryman continued.

Jarmin admitted that he and Matthews started talking about drugs (crack cocaine) and women. Matthews told him that if he would let him use his wife's car, he'd bring back some girls and some crack for a party. The agreeable Jarmin gave Matthews the keys. Matthews drove off and never came back.

Jarmin was angry and decided to do something about it. He went over to where Matthews was living with his brother, Martin, who told him that Matthews had been found dead. That's when Jarmin filed the report with the police about his wife's missing car. As for Matthews, all Jarmin remembered was that the last time he saw Matthews, he was wearing blue jeans, a red shirt, a baseball cap, and white tennis shoes.

He was alone.

The details seemed mundane, but they weren't. It was a way to backtrack Matthews's movements leading up to his killing. After the phone call, police canvassed the street Jarmin had spoken of and wound up speaking to Calvin Early. Early said that on Friday, October 8, an unknown white male, two unknown white females, and Larry Matthews showed up at his residence in a silver car. Early's description of the white male fit Jarmin.

"They all entered my house," Early said, "and they drank and played cards for a while. After a while, Larry left walking away, I don't know where. Larry never returned."

A day later, police spotted the stolen car and pulled it over. As soon as they did, the car's doors sprung open and four men ran from it, with the surprised police at the scene unable to catch up with them. The car was then processed for evidence, at which time a few latent fingerprints were recovered.

When Jarmin went to the impound lot to claim his car, the St. Charles cops decided to go there and chat with him again. Jarmin made the same statement that he had previously given to the Houma Police. Again he was hesitant, this time admitting he was nervous because he was on parole for drug charges and didn't want to get in trouble with his probation officer.

Regardless, police now knew that sometime after Larry Matthews drove away from Jarmin's place in his wife's car, he fell into the clutches of . . . a cocaine overdose. He had officially succumbed to a white powder, not a guy with strong hands.

"Due to this information, I will close this case, taking no further actions at this time, closing it as an accidental overdose," Jerome wrote in his report.

Wendy Guidry was just trying to make a living like everyone else. She and her husband, Dirk, owned Gator Storage, a hundred-unit storage-rental facility in town. The Gator had no visible security—no electronic gate or security codes like some storage facilities had. Perhaps the couple figured that, being in a rural area, there was very little chance of theft.

All of the units were sealed with dull blue shuttered doors that stood out starkly against the cane field surrounding the facility. Guidry had received a report from one of her employees about a strange smell coming from one of the units. Once she arrived, she too smelled the stink immediately, noticing a dark fluid seeping out from under the door of an unlocked unit.

Unlike all the other units, which were padlocked, this one was secured by a simple twist tie. Guidry removed the tie and lifted the door warily. The stench was overwhelming and the dark fluid was now readily visible in the light of day as blood. That's when her gaze centered on the body. The man was laid on his back, naked, and looked middle-aged, maybe in his fifties.

Guidry panicked and bolted from the unit. When she got back to her office, she dialed 911. Within minutes, Houma police arrived on the scene, followed by the Terrebonne Parish detectives, who had also been summoned. Detective Simon Fryman of the Houma Police Department and Detective Dawn Bergeron of the Terrebonne Parish Sheriff's Office were led to the unit, where they found the body in an advanced state of decomposition.

As the criminalists began their work, Bergeron and Fryman peppered Wendy Guidry with questions. How had she initially come to make the call? Why had she gone to that specific storage bin? Then they asked Guidry to give them a complete list of all the rental units, including tenants' names, addresses, and phone numbers.

The police then called every single name on that list—more than fifty people—to find out if anyone had noticed anything out of the ordinary. No such luck. No one had seen, heard, or smelled anything unusual. Once again, it was as if the killer had drifted into thin air.

The next day, the *Houma Daily Courier* carried a front-page article about the body's discovery. The police had decided there was no point in embargoing the story. The article went so far as to link this fresh kill with the others that had preceded it, speculating that a serial killer targeting men was on the loose.

However, the Associated Press did not pick up the story, so word of the new murder failed to be disseminated beyond the Southern Louisiana area. Pending identification of the decomposed "John Doe," the coroner found "no obvious signs of trauma to the body." The decomp was too far along to tell much else. The victim was kept refrigerated in the morgue until he could be positively identified.

The next morning, Bergeron returned to speak with Wendy Guidry. Bergeron had a hunch that further questioning might elicit new information. Many times, witnesses remember more when they repeat their statements. Guidry's recollection was that one of her employees, Rod Billings, was someplace at the back of the property on Saturday, two days prior to the discovery of the body.

Bergeron found Billings in the office. He explained that he had been in back sweeping out the cobwebs from the climate-controlled units. He didn't see anything out of the ordinary.

The next day, a local merchant named Francis Barber came into the Houma Police Department to report that his childhood friend, Michael Barnett, was missing. Barber had last seen Barnett on Friday evening as he was leaving 317 Ruth Street. He was on his bicycle. Barnett told Barber that he was going to meet a girl at a fire station.

Detectives showed Barber a picture a sketch artist had drawn the previous day. The decomposition of the body was far along, but not so far as to prevent at least partial identification. The artist had noticed a unique dragon tattoo on the decedent's arm and drew it in detail. They showed the tattoo sketch to Barber.

"Yup," said Barber, nodding. "I am positively sure Michael had that tattoo. I remember seeing it many times."

So now they had an identification. While Detective Fryman continued to take Barber's statement, Bergeron went to the fire station. Barber had said that Barnett was on his way to a "fire station" to meet a girl. Unfortunately, the firemen had seen nothing out of the ordinary. It seemed Barnett had not made it to the firehouse.

The killer was murdering mostly black men, but he had also started killing Caucasians. The detectives pooled information and someone said that Michael Barnett had a brother named David who was possibly living on Miranda Court. They got back in their cars and drove to Miranda Court, a run-down neighborhood of detached homes. No one was home at the brother's address.

They left a message on the door for the brother to call and went back to headquarters. One hour later, Barnett's friend Jack Gilings called. Just about the same time, David Barnett got the message and called too. The detectives asked the men to come down to be interviewed. They both had the same story.

They said they'd last seen Barnett approximately four weeks ago. They had gotten into an argument, in which they accused Barnett of stealing power tools from Gilings. Both men had on-again, off-again friendships with Barnett.

"However, he's still family," David Barnett said.

No longer angry with Michael Barnett, they were very concerned he had been reported missing. Both men claimed that Michael's new roommate, Dorian Bates, may have been involved. Detectives made a note of Bates's name and explained that Barnett had not been positively identified yet. They were trying to use fingerprints and dental records to aid in positive identification. The tattoo wasn't enough.

After he got home later in the day, David Barnett remembered a few things. He called and spoke with Bergeron, filling her in on his brother's background. Michael was born in Mississippi, and his biological mother gave him to Chad and Patricia Barnett for adoption. David, thirty-five years old, was their biological son.

"Michael was raised as a brother to me," David added.

Bergeron told Barnett of the advanced state of decomposition, which made positive identification difficult. Anxious to help catch his brother's killer, he volunteered to help police check Mississippi for possible dental records. Then Bergeron found a judge who agreed to sign a search warrant. Armed with the warrant, she drove over to the Ruth Street apartment where Barnett lived and went through the place. She was trying to locate items that might have belonged to Michael Barnett.

The hope was that they could take prints off something he'd touched and match them to the ones they had gotten off the body. Several pieces of mail and a few CDs were collected and taken to the department for processing. The next day, Bergeron was looking through Barnett's correspondence when she discovered that he had been housed as a child in the Baptist Children's Village in Jackson, Mississippi.

Maybe he'd seen a dentist while there. She faxed a request to see Barnett's dental records. Soon, the fax machine rang and the pages started coming through. Barnett had seen a Dr. Don Murphy on February 8, 1999, when Barnett was a teenager. Calling Murphy's office, Bergeron learned that Murphy had retired and a Dr. Mike Madison had taken over the business.

Madison's office still had the old records. Soon, she received hard copies of the dental records in the mail. They were turned over to the coroner's office for comparison to the victim. The coroner confirmed that the deceased was definitely Michael Barnett. With a positive identification, Bergeron shared the news with David Barnett and Jack Gilings: Michael was dead.

Gilings and Barnett urged Bergeron to question Michael's roommate, whom they continued to suspect.

Dawn Bergeron had been coming through the ranks. Major Vernon Bourgeois, who was the overall field commander of the Terrebonne Parish Sheriff's Office, had been watching her for some time.

"She's a real firecracker!" he'd exclaim to anyone who asked.

The ambivalent high school graduate who wasn't sure what she was going to do with her life had grown into a no-nonsense, dedicated, intelligent, and—most importantly—empathetic detective. Empathy was the one thing any good detective needed—the ability to put yourself in the suspect's shoes and relate to what he's feeling when being questioned.

Bergeron just seemed to be a natural at getting confessions, or as police like to call them, statements. Her personal life had also gone through important changes. She'd married, given birth to a daughter, divorced the child's father, then gotten remarried, this time to a detective like herself. In spite of the domestic obligations of being a wife and mother, Bergeron remained dedicated to her job.

She was known to beg off social functions with her daughter because "Mommy had to serve a warrant." It was this combination of being a sympathetic parent and a committed cop that made her especially good on the job.

Going through all the names on the list Guidry had given them of people who had rented storage units, Bergeron came up with a blank. There was no connection with anyone on the list to Barnett. Bergeron, though, was well aware of the Southern Louisiana serial killer. She wondered if Barnett could have been one of his victims.

CHAPTER TEN

DIRT BIKES AT DUSK

Terrebonne Parish, February 2005

It was another sleepless night for Dennis Thornton. There had been many of these, as he struggled to see what he hadn't yet: some piece of evidence, some clue, that would lead him to the killer.

He had heard of the Matthews murder and the grisly discovery of Barnett's body. In the latter case, the coroner could not establish cause of death because the decomposition was too well along. Despite that failure, and the failure to link conclusively the Matthews and Barnett cases to the serial killer, behind the scenes, the detectives strongly suspected they were related.

He didn't pause to consider the guy's "kill total" and where he stood in US criminal history. That, however would have provided some perspective, not to mention a great story for any reporter smart enough to pay attention. Had they compared their killer's total number of victims, the Louisiana cops would have discovered that their murderer was in distinguished company.

Dominique had now killed as many as Jeffrey Dahmer, a.k.a. "the Milwaukee Cannibal," with fifteen murders. Unless he was caught quickly, he would exceed that. But as far as the detectives were concerned, they had an unknown serial killer on their hands who moved freely from parish to parish, leaving a trail of bodies behind him.

Now he appeared to be concentrating on Terrebonne Parish. It was therefore a logical assumption that he was living someplace in the parish, which appeared to be his "comfort zone." Some serial killers would remain forever at large were it not for some subconscious action, usually a slight mistake, that lead the police to them.

Long Island serial killer Joel Rifkin, for example, was spotted by police because there was a body part hanging out the back door of his van. Some may even expose themselves deliberately. Ted Bundy was a lousy driver. His erratic driving led to his arrest twice, the second time after he had escaped . . . for the second time!

In cases where the cops don't know whodunit, suspects are brought in for questioning. But suspicions are not enough, so suspects are released if there isn't evidence of their guilt. Then, after committing more murders and getting away with them, the serial killer will often confess to his crimes. Kendall Francois, a.k.a. "the Poughkeepsie Serial Killer," was originally brought in for questioning and even passed a lie-detector test. After a victim escaped his clutches in 1998, he was brought in again for questioning. This time, he couldn't keep his mouth shut and confessed to killing eight women and using his house as a "body dump."

Admissions of this kind have nothing to do with getting it off your conscience; serial killers don't have one. Otherwise they couldn't do what they do. No—the confession is a boast of what he has done. Sometimes a confession can even be used to save a killer's life. Attorney Clarence Darrow showed that in the Leopold and Loeb case.

First he got the thrill-killers to plead guilty to murdering little Bobby Franks, and then he argued for their lives before the trial judge. Darrow opposed the death penalty. In the end, the judge sided with Darrow and spared the murderers' lives instead of hanging them. But in that case, both suspects emerged quickly. Here, investigators did not know who the killer was, but they knew he was smart.

Forensically aware, he didn't leave anything behind. That made the job more difficult. What was it that made him kill at some times and not at others? Thornton was unable to answer that question. He also couldn't figure out how the killer picked up his victims or talked them into trusting him. The questions continued to swirl around in his mind, unanswered.

The Houma Shrine Center, or "club" as the locals referred to it, was located right in front of the air base. Everyone called it "the air base," but it was actually a small airport, used primarily by oil companies with offices in the Houma area. The Shrine Center itself, which one passed before getting to the air base, was a wooden clapboard building, weathered enough to say, encouragingly, that it had seen better days. Their origins tracing back to 1870, the Shriners had by the twenty-first century become an international club devoted to "good works" through its Shriners Hospital.

Behind the Shrine Center was an open grassy field leading up to a forest. The whole area was deserted at night. It was evening, February 19, 2005, and the Shrine Center looked ghostly. The field behind it was just a sheet of solid black darkness—until it was suddenly lit up by the headlights of Dominique's Sonoma. He knew the place because he'd read the meter there; no one noticed him or his automobile.

The next day, Steve Pym and his son, Vincent, decided to go to the air base to ride their dirt bikes. As they were loading the bikes, friend Donald Clendenon showed up to visit, then asked to go along. So Pym threw in a third dirt bike, and off they went for a few hours of riding.

The three had been dirt biking around the Shriners building and airfield a short while when Clendenon caught a flash of clothing in the grass. On closer inspection, he saw that the clothes were actually covering a body and set off instantly to tell Pym. Pym was startled by his urgency. Up ahead, Clendenon was riding toward him wildly, waving him down.

Pym reached Clendenon first, who frantically explained the situation. Pym turned fast and shouted at his son, who attempted to follow.

"Stay away!"

Pym followed Clendenon back to the body. When Clendenon started to reach down, Pym said, "No. If the guy's drunk, he might get up fighting."

Pym had seen a beer bottle in a tree. To him, it looked like the guy had just passed out. Then again, he didn't have a shirt on. Also, he was wearing jeans and socks, but no shoes. Clendenon stooped down to see if the stranger was still breathing. He didn't appear to be. His wrists and back looked blue; flies were swarming around him.

Pym pulled out his cell phone. In the eight years Dominique had been operating, cell phones had become a common pocket item. Pym dialed 911.

"I want to report the discovery of a body."

He gave their location, then waited for police. Next, Pym dialed his mother to come pick up his son. He needed his kid away from the scene. The last thing any child needs to see is a dead body.

Once again Detective Simon Fryman of the Houma Police Department got the call at home.

"Respond to the rear of the Shriner Building on Moffett Road, in reference to a body that has been discovered," the dispatcher instructed.

Fryman drove down to the site, wondering what it was this time. He was met by uniformed officers who led him to the crime scene. Fryman saw the white male laying on his side. He was wearing only blue jeans and socks. The Houma Police Department Crime Scene Division began to search the area for possible clues. The forensic photographer took his photographs of the body and all the other potential evidence of a crime.

Examining the body from the rear, Fryman saw nothing that indicated a weapon had been used. As in other homicide investigations in his parish, Fryman himself bagged the left hand of the victim and began doing the same thing to the other hand, when he stopped cold. Not only did he recognize the victim; he knew him!

It was when Fryman moved the victim's right arm back from his face, to bag the hand, that he saw that it was Leon Lirette. Fryman had dealt with Lirette in the murder of Noka Jones, not to mention the fact that he had arrested him for previous low-level offenses.

How had he wound up here?

"I'll see you later, T-Paul," he said, and walked out the door.

That, as Leon Lirette had told police three years earlier, was the last thing Noka Jones had ever said to him. Now, in a terrible act of fate, it appeared that Lirette had died in the same manner as his friend. Fryman continued to bag the right hand. That's when he noticed several small wounds on Lirette's chest.

He also noted what appeared to be markings on Lirette's neck, possibly left by some kind of ligature used to suffocate him. Maybe it was the same killer as before? There were small particles of blood, a dried-cranberry color, spattered across the body. Blood pooled from Lirette's nostrils.

The shoeless feet were bagged. Another detective ran a vacuum sweep on Lirette's blue jeans for trace evidence. It was just a small cordless vacuum with a high-tech filtering system. It could sometimes yield valuable evidence, like fibers and skin scrapings.

The body was taken to the Terrebonne Parish morgue for autopsy, but Fryman had more urgent matters to address. Rather than join detectives at the station, he drove straight to Lirette's house on State Street, an address Fryman had become familiar with after a series of busts. Lirette lived with his mother, who answered the door and consented to a preliminary search of the premises.

Pointing to blood at the rear of the living room behind the recliner, she was panicked that her son might be hurt or even dead. Fryman also saw a thumb-sized bloodstain on the recliner itself. He realized that proceeding any further without a search warrant was constitutionally unsound. Warrant in hand two hours later, Fryman went back to Lirette's residence.

The neighborhood Lirette had lived in was a drug-infested area. Along with a team of investigators, Fryman entered the living room, where the processing of evidence began. Fryman waited it out until the specialists did their job, at which time the scene was released and turned over to Lirette's mother.

Fryman thought it possible that the blood was Lirette's; that could be confirmed later in the day with laboratory analysis.

For now, Fryman continued his investigation into Lirette's background, hoping he might find some clue to his death. He interviewed one of Lirette's friends, Mark Donaldson, who referred to him by his nickname, "T-Paul."

The last time Donaldson had seen T-Paul was about six days ago, Tuesday of last week, at Laverne's Bar, by the Bryson Mobil station. He was in the bar drinking when T-Paul tried to come in carrying a forty-ounce beer. He was denied entrance. T-Paul left it outside and was then allowed to come in. Donaldson bought Lirette a beer and they drank together. After that, T-Paul left.

Nobody had talked to him since, and friends were worried. Donaldson gave Fryman a description of what T-Paul had been wearing when he last saw him: white muscle T-shirt, blue jeans, and a red beanie cap. Fryman immediately sought out Joey Gazzo, who was the last person to speak to Lirette before he was murdered.

The fifty-three-year-old filled in some blanks. Gazzo had seen Lirette for the last time on the previous Thursday at Lirette's house. He and Donaldson had stayed over for the night. Lirette's mother, Dorothy, was at home. Gazzo and Donaldson got up that morning and went to work with Mark's brother Darrell of D&M Roofing. They came home about 5:30 p.m.

A short while later, he and Mark went out to go to the store to get a beer and ended up at Laverne's Bar. He had a beer and then went to the Pit Stop to get something to eat. When he got home, T-Paul called.

"I answered the telephone and he asked me to talk to his mother. He said he was drunk, stoned, and did not know where he was. Then, all of a sudden, the phone went dead."

Donaldson figured it was about 9 p.m. He also figured that T-Paul hung up the phone, or that someone did it for him.

"The next time I saw Mark was the next morning when we went to work. We did not talk about T-Paul at all."

After not hearing from her son for a few days, Lirette's mother had gotten worried and called the police. In chatting further with the detective, Gazzo came to recall something else.

"A couple of nights ago, Mark and Dorothy had an argument. Mark was drunk and he made a comment to Dorothy that the police might find her son dead. But I think it was the alcohol talking."

It probably was. There was no indication that Mark Donaldson was involved in Leon Lirette's disappearance and murder. Fryman found Lirette's movements hard to trace because he moved around the street a lot. Yet the two interviews brought out important information. Lirette had made a phone call at a time that looked to be immediately before his death, or close to it.

He was heavily under the influence. Fryman figured that, with his judgment impaired, Lirette was vulnerable. Easily enticed, a plum target for a serial killer out trolling for his next victim. The next day, Fryman received a call from a clerk at the Bryson Mobil store. The clerk, who had heard of the investigation, told him to contact Diedre Porter. She might have some information about Leon Lirette's disappearance.

Fryman called Porter, who also worked at the Bryson store. She told him that on either Monday or Tuesday, which would have been February 14 or 15, she had seen Leon Lirette during daylight hours speaking to a white male, about twenty years old, in a bright-purple eighties-model car with rims.

"I don't actually know Leon Lirette. He was just a guy who came to the store," Porter explained to the detective.

Porter was implying, however tangentially, that a white guy in a bright-purple muscle car from the 1980s was somehow involved in Lirette's disappearance. While it seemed doubtful—serial killers don't generally have vehicles that stand out; the idea is to blend in—every tip needed to be noted and checked out. But the first thing was the autopsy.

Fryman went over to the coroner's office to attend the autopsy, which Dr. Garcia was in the process of performing. A sexual-assault kit was prepared and the results were turned over to Fryman for forensic analysis. Noting that the victim had been dead for about twenty-four to thirty-six hours, Garcia looked at the eyes. There was hemorrhaging in both of them.

In Dr. Garcia's professional opinion, "the victim was extremely drunk at the time of death and it would not have taken much force to strangle him."

Fryman went back to the department feeling that the autopsy had only confirmed what they already knew: it was the work of their serial killer. Dr. Garcia was very straightfor-ward—Lirette had been strangled to death in the same manner as the previous victims. The detective wondered if being drunk had in some way softened his death.

Before he had a chance to sit down at his desk, another detective told Fryman that a black female and a white male had come in for an interview on an unrelated case. They had both once resided at the Sugar Bowl Motel. Fryman knew the Sugar Bowl was a notorious place for pickups. Male and female prostitutes lived there and worked the large street right in front of it.

Fryman reasoned that Lirette might have been down there looking for some action when the wrong person picked him up. Soon, the woman identified herself as Marie Maples. Fryman pulled out a mug shot of Leon Lirette and handed it to Maples.

"I don't know his name, but I'm a hundred percent sure I seen him in the parking lot of the Sugar Bowl last week."

That was four days before his body was discovered. Garcia had said he could have been dead up to thirty-six hours before discovery. That left one day to account for.

"I lived at the Sugar Bowl Motel for approximately one year," Maples continued. "While living there, I became familiar with several 'subjects' that frequented the place. That guy in the picture you showed me, I last seen him in a white, older-model Suburban with another white guy."

"What was Lirette wearing?"

"A white T-shirt with white underwear under it, baggy blue jeans, and a red cap turned sideways."

The white T-shirt had vanished. Lirette had been shirtless when found, and no T-shirt had been located on or near the dump site.

"The Suburban pulled up next to Laverne's Bar," Maples continued.

Laverne's Bar was near the motel. According to Maples, the man in the picture got out of the truck, which had out-of-town plates. She couldn't remember what state they were from.

"When the guy got out of the truck, the other white guy behind the wheel kept hurrying him up. He kept telling him that the police was looking for him and they needed to leave."

Maples claimed that her memory of the person shown in the picture was so vivid because she had said to herself that he was acting like a "nigger." It was the way he was dressed and how he carried himself, as if that justified the use of the "n" word. She also said that a black woman named Susan Prindle hung out with the white guy who was driving the Suburban.

"Prindle usually frequented room 234 or 235 at the Sugar Bowl," she said.

Maples was a nosy person who obviously paid attention not only to her business, but to others' as well.

According to Maples, there was a short white man with a mustache in one of the rooms. The second room was occupied by an older black male. As for the white truck, it usually came to the Sugar Bowl late at night. Maples said that she had seen the white Suburban recently.

The white guy had worn a red cap. He had a busted lip and it looked like it had been busted for quite some time.

"He walked with a limp," she said.

Fryman had heard enough. He handed Maples his business card and asked her to call if she remembered anything else.

A white guy with a limp?

Detectives know that murder brings out the aberrant tendencies in people. They like to say they saw something, or believe they saw something, that is relevant to the case, if only for the attention. It was through that filter investigators needed to process incoming information.

The *Houma Courier* ran a story of the discovery of Lirette's body; most of Houma's residents didn't care. The paper would routinely report such murders when they occurred. The guy was just some hustler who got in over his head. It was bound to happen sooner or later, considering the kind of lifestyle Leon Lirette had led.

That night, while patrolling the east side of Houma, Fryman saw a white Chevrolet Suburban on Chateau Court. But the man behind the wheel was black, not white as Maples had described. As he approached the mini-mart to pay for gas, Fryman parked his car and followed on foot. He showed the man his badge and asked for his ID.

The man identified himself as Lloyd Peck and his ID confirmed it. He was surprised the cop was questioning him because he hadn't done anything illegal.

"Do you know a man named Leon Lirette?" Fryman asked.

"No," said Peck.

"Do you allow anyone else to utilize your vehicle?"

"No."

Fryman then quickly explained the reason Peck had been stopped. Peck completely understood. Fryman also warned Peck that he might be stopped again in the future and recommended that he comply with law enforcement. Of course, Peck agreed. Before Fryman released the man, he looked in the window of the suburban and noticed that the entire rear seat was filled with boxes.

He made a mental note and released Peck.

On March 3, Fryman was contacted by Captain Malcolm Wolfe of the Terrebonne Parish Sheriff's Office. Wolfe told Fryman that the sister of one of his investigators had witnessed an individual on the air base on February 19 "that appeared to be extremely nervous." That nervous individual was in a maroon car, possibly in the same area where Leon Lirette's body was located.

The next day, the investigator in question, Brittany Johnson, called Fryman to follow up. She explained that once her sister Susan Idle had learned that a body was recovered at the air base, she told her that a suspicious guy in a car had parked near a large tree by the Houma Shriners building. Fryman called the sister in and asked Brittany to join them.

According to Susan Idle, "While on Moffett Road, we passed the church, which is next to the Shriners building, then the Shriners building, when I saw the maroon car parked next to a tree. It was either a Buick or Chrysler. A white guy was standing on the driver's side doorway of the car and appeared nervous as he gazed at the passing traffic.

"He was smoking a cigarette and he was dressed in a white T-shirt with writing on it, blue jeans and like a normal haircut. As soon as I heard about the body being found on the air base, I called my sister."

"A normal haircut?" What did that mean? Fryman took Idle over to the air base to reconstruct where she had been, where the car had been parked, and most importantly, where the victim had been dumped. Idle's account brought the cops one step closer to the serial killer, though they didn't know it yet. As for Dominique, his choice of victim had once again worked to his advantage.

There was a serial killer running amok in Southern Louisiana and no one knew it was him. He was acting like he could get away with it forever.

CHAPTER ELEVEN

THE WHITE VAN

Lafourche, Jefferson, and Terrebonne Parishes, April 2005

In his mug shot, August Watkins looked like a real tough guy.

He glared at the camera, his expression stony and defiant. In death, his expression was totally passive. His fully clothed body lay in a wooded area near the Lafourche Work Release Center in Lafourche Parish, discovered by a passing motorist who immediately called the sheriff's office.

The response of detectives was immediate. But once again, there was no identification on the victim. The Lafourche Parish Sheriff's Office put out a BOLO bulletin containing information describing the victim, seeking help from other parishes in identifying him. Two days later, on April 11, Fryman's lieutenant handed him a copy of the BOLO.

Looking it over, he saw the similarity to the victims in his parish and theorized it was the same killer. Fryman then called the Lafourche Parish Sheriff's Office with the news of the serial killer he was trailing.

"Detective John Walker is currently investigating the incident," Fryman was told by a receptionist who was authorized to speak. "He is currently at the Jefferson Parish Coroner's Office attending the victim's autopsy."

"Have you made an identification yet on the body?" Fryman asked.

"Not at the moment," the receptionist stated. "I'll have him call you during the day with particulars on the investigation."

Ty Hutchins, a tall, lanky detective, got back to Fryman later in the day. The coroner had ruled that the victim's manner of death was strangulation. The victim's identity would be shared with Fryman as soon as Hutchins got it. A few more hours went by. Toward the end of the day, Hutchins took a drive and walked in the door of the Houma Police Department.

He met with Fryman and told him that they had gotten prints off the corpse. Run through the AFIS database, August Terrell Watkins was finally identified as the victim. Watkins was a thirty-two-year-old black man. He had brown eyes, was five feet six inches tall, and weighed 130 pounds.

"We have a possible address for him," Hutchins told Fryman. "Also, a next of kin. An aunt Pearl Nixon's address."

Fryman filled him in on his investigation. On the basis of the choice of victim and the MO, Fryman suspected they were hunting the same man—the Southern Louisiana serial killer. The two detectives drove to Watkins's last known address on Isabel Street. It was possible he had been abducted from that location or near there; there might be some clues. Maybe something left behind.

Arriving, they knocked at the door. It was opened by an attractive woman in her thirties. After the detectives showed her their shields, she volunteered information.

"My name is Sandra Hooten," she said.

When Hooten was told whom they were looking for, she motioned behind her.

"August lived behind me. It's the last house on the left," she said. "But I don't think he's there."

"Why?" Hutchins asked.

"He was evicted a couple of months ago. I think he was sent to live with some relatives," Hooten answered.

Fryman walked to the rear of the residence. There were two other houses behind the one Hooten lived in. A look in the window where Watkins had lived revealed the home to be completely empty. Fryman and Hutchins then decided to go over to the second address they had, on Harding Street, for Pearl Nixon, next of kin.

When the cops arrived, they were told by a neighbor that Pearl Nixon had just left to get a tire fixed. After a while, the detectives saw a gray Dodge Neon heading their way. They thought the driver could be Pearl Nixon. She pulled to the curb and cut the ignition. Getting out, she walked around the car, and Hutchins approached her.

"Pearl?"

The middle-aged woman looked up and saw the detective's badge.

"I'm Detective Hutchins. I'm sorry to have to tell you this, but your nephew, Terrell Watkins, is unfortunately dead."

While Hutchins was speaking to the woman, Fryman, on a hunch, had wandered up Harding Street to another residence, where he encountered an elderly black woman named . . . Pearl Nixon. Suddenly, he realized that by some strange coincidence, the woman Hutchins was talking to was named Pearl all right, but not Pearl Nixon.

But Fryman didn't pause to relay the info to Hutchins. He immediately began his interview with Nixon.

"I'm August Watkins's aunt," Nixon explained to Fryman. "The family usually calls him 'Terrell.'"

"Did you know he was living on Peters Street?"

"Yes, but I learned that he couldn't pay his rent and was put out by the landlord."

She also said that he was later living with Mina Parker on Matthews Drive, but she wasn't sure if he still was there.

Then Hutchins, who had just been informed of the mix-up, arrived. The questioning continued.

"When was the last time you saw Terrell?"

"Here, in my place," said Nixon. "But he was behind my house, at Susan Sisto's house. I was watching television and I overheard Terrell say, 'Auntie, I'm leaving.'"

She said he was carrying a black garbage bag and a duffel bag. That was the last time she saw him. She had no memory of what her nephew had been wearing. Fryman and Hutchins left Nixon and went over to Susan Sisto's house in the rear. Sisto told them that Watkins had come to her house on Friday morning around 8 a.m.

The place was a mess, and Watkins, who lived with Sisto, had made it that way. And when he arrived, Sisto gave Watkins a garbage bag—not for cleaning up the mess, but to use as luggage. It contained some clothes she'd received from various people that she figured he could use; he didn't have much. She didn't know of anyone he hung with and she was sure he had left her place in the daytime. He was probably homeless.

As the detectives continued their conversation, Elizabeth Jones showed up. She too was an aunt of Watkins and was in shock after hearing about her nephew's death. Another nephew,

John Reed, had told her that he had seen Terrell walking through the Houma Tunnel, a dirty, smelly pedestrian tunnel that leads from one side of town to the other. According to Reed, Terrell had been holding a garbage bag when he went through.

Other relatives then began to arrive as the news of Watkins's murder spread. Family friend Carrie Prescott said that she had spoken to Watkins recently. He had left the house where he'd been living with his girlfriend because her kids were getting on his nerves. A woman was waiting for him outside when he did. Prescott couldn't remember anything distinctive about the woman and had no idea who she was.

A second friend of Watkins's, Sandy Smithers, told Detectives Walker and Fryman that her niece Francine Scott had found a garbage bag in the woods near Jack's Grocery. She wondered if maybe it was Terrell's. The detectives headed out to investigate. It was possible, they theorized, that Watkins had been abducted near the grocery store and someone might have seen something.

When they got to Jack's Grocery, the two detectives got out of their car and walked toward the entrance. They were about to enter when Francine Scott appeared and directed them to an empty lot to the left of the bar Tim Buc II. There, Scott showed them the bag she had found. Fryman saw that it was near a tree within a small wooded area that led to an open field.

Walker noticed a partial watchband hanging from a tree. Perhaps it was the serial killer's. Calling in the criminalists, the scene was photographed, the bag and the watchband tagged as evidence, and the area scoured—with no notable results. Back at the Houma Police Department headquarters that afternoon, Fryman looked through the case file, trying to spot something he might have missed previously.

It was frustrating. When would they finally catch the killer?

Near the end of his shift in late afternoon, Fryman was patrolling the streets of Houma. What he hadn't told anybody was that he had previously "popped" the other nephew, John Railsback, on a drug offense. So when he eyeballed Railsback driving a Plymouth, Fryman stopped him to chat. Railsback said that he had last seen Watkins on Friday evening, April 8.

It was right after he had gotten off work from his job at the Cleaner Than New detail shop. He claimed that, after being forced to move out by his girlfriend, Terrell was homeless. That's how Railsback came to find him sleeping on the steps to the Houma Tunnel. Railsback recalled that Watkins carried a dark-colored duffel bag and a garbage bag with red string.

Fryman asked Railsback to come in for an interview the next day. Railsback gave a formal statement, explaining he was getting off work on Friday, April 8, 2005.

"It was approximately 5 p.m. or 6 p.m. when I started walking toward the Houma Tunnel, toward my home. When I got to the stairs, I saw Terrell sleeping on the lower level of the eastside entrance steps."

"Why were you sleeping in the tunnel?" he had asked his cousin.

"Liz Jones put me out of her house," Terrell answered. "I didn't have anywhere to go."

"Why don't you go back to Elizabeth's? You shouldn't be sleeping in the tunnel."

Railsback had finished his conversation with his cousin. Then he had continued to walk through the tunnel toward Margaret Street.

"I went to Elizabeth Jones's residence after talking with you yesterday," Railsback said to Fryman. "She told me about a white man in a white truck that was looking for Terrell. I'm going back to see if I can get some information on the white truck. If I get anything, I'll contact you."

Fryman wasn't content with that response. It was necessary to trace the last steps of the victim to establish the timeline of death. Fryman had Railsback drive out to the Houma Tunnel, where Fryman took photographs of the area. The detective saw several articles of trash, but none appeared to have anything to do with the disappearance or homicide of Watkins.

Returning to Jack's Grocery, Fryman decided to interview the clerk, Tabitha Zwerling. He showed her a picture of August Watkins. She recognized him, and then some. She was family.

"August Watkins's brother, Willie Saulsberry, lives with me. I remember Terrell coming in the store on Friday morning. He purchased two Little Debbie iced honey buns and one Diet Coke. I didn't see him carrying anything, but I do remember him saying the honey buns were not for him, because he is a diabetic."

Zwerling said that she had heard Terrell was dead. It got her thinking about who might have done it. Willie had told her that Watkins hung out with a white guy, though Willie didn't know his name. Watkins had said the white guy was a friend of his.

"The guy drove a white truck. Willie also told me that Terrell talked about having a girlfriend in Thibodaux. We thought he was making that up. Willie had never met the girl, but Terrell talked about her constantly."

Fryman's cell phone rang. Excusing himself, he took the call and spoke to someone from dispatch. Elizabeth Jones had been calling the department repeatedly, requesting to speak with him. Ending the interview with Zwerling prematurely, Fryman went over to Matthews Drive to meet her.

"Terrell used to live with me but just recently, he moved out," Jones said. "I have a new boyfriend, John Bolden, who is coming home soon."

Watkins had said that he was going to live with his new girl-friend, "Winter." She didn't know Winter's last name.

"But she is a short, fat black girl," she added.

The next day, Terrell came back at about ten in the morning. He was looking for his social security check and Jones gave it to him. They went to Regions Bank on Grand Caillou Road. Since Terrell didn't have enough money for an account of his own, she deposited his check in her account and gave him the cash, common practice in impoverished communities.

Driving back to her house, Watkins asked Jones to let him get out of the car at the intersection. She pulled over to the curb and he got out. She never saw him again.

"When I got home, the telephone rang and it was the white guy calling for Terrell."

Fryman asked how she knew who it was.

"He said on the phone that he was Terrell's friend, that he has the white truck."

Jones remembered coming home from Mount Pilgrim Church on Sunday, April 10, at about 10:30 a.m. She saw a white truck on the road: behind the wheel appeared to be a heavy-set man wearing a hat. Seated on the passenger side of the truck was a black woman she knew as Winter. As the truck passed, both of them looked toward her house in what she thought to be an odd manner.

Fryman was on to something—or so he thought.

He began to theorize that maybe the killer was the man driving the white vehicle, that maybe, finally, this would lead them to the serial killer. Suddenly, the door opened and John Bolden, Jones's new boyfriend, arrived home from work. Fryman quickly explained that he was there investigating Terrell Watkins's death, and it turned out Bolden also knew him.

"When was the last time you saw Terrell?" Fryman asked him.

"Friday, April 8, standing on St. Joseph Street near an abandoned green house. Elizabeth had sent me to the Family Food Mart on St. Joseph Street. Everyone calls it the 'Chinese' store."

"What time was that?"

Bolden figured it was about 9:30 p.m., when he saw Terrell and the woman standing there.

"Did you see a white truck that day?"

He said that he hadn't.

Fryman put out a BOLO on the white truck. Dispatch soon informed him that the vehicle he was searching for, that he hoped contained his serial killer at the wheel, was back at Jack's Grocery. When he got to Jack's, the detective saw a white truck with green trim leaving the lot. He could see a man at the wheel.

Excited, Fryman swung the wheel around sharply, turned on his siren, and gave chase. The siren pierced through the din of a too-ordinary day. The blue, white, and red lights that flashed from his car were intimidating enough to make even Bonnie and Clyde pull over, which the driver of the truck did. Quickly, Fryman ran the truck's Louisiana plate through the state's motor-vehicle database.

Up came the owner's name: Maggie Brown.

Fryman wore a sport jacket, which he flicked to the side, putting his hand on the butt of his 9mm. Sauntering slowly up to the driver's side, he saw that the driver wasn't Maggie Brown—of that he was positive. He was a man wearing eyeglasses and a hat. Sitting next to him in the passenger seat was a woman, possibly Maggie Brown.

Fryman showed the driver his badge and asked him to step out of the vehicle. He thought he might have his serial killer. Fryman put him up firmly against the side of the truck, frisked him, and then snapped on the handcuffs.

"You have the right to remain silent. Anything you say may be used against you in a court of law. You have the right to the presence of an attorney. If you cannot afford one, one will be appointed by the court. Do you understand these rights?"

"Yes," the driver said.

"You're not under arrest at this point," Fryman informed him. "But I need to talk to you in reference to an investigation."

The driver relaxed a little, though he shouldn't have. Once a cop puts on the cuffs, advises you of your rights, and won't let you go, you are effectively under arrest. He identified himself as Michael Joselyn, date of birth June 2, 1958. But his driver's license said his name was Jack Pennington. Taking this discrepancy into careful consideration, Fryman confiscated his license as evidence and placed him in the back seat of his car. As for the woman, she was a twenty-something, Selma Davies.

"I don't know why we were stopped," she said as Fryman escorted her to his car.

But she did, or thought she did.

"I know my uncle Mike has a drug problem. I think he gets his drugs from a family called Jones," she volunteered.

Another police car arrived on the scene and Davies was taken in for further questioning. She told Fryman that her uncle Mike picked her up to accompany him to a notary to witness some documents he needed to sign. Then they went to Jack's Grocery to get some gas.

Showing her Mike's driver's license, Fryman asked her, "Why does your uncle's ID say that he's Jack Pennington from Missouri?"

She looked at it.

"I don't know why," she finally answered. "But the picture is actually him."

Detectives typed up Davies's statement, had her sign it, and released her. Now they turned their attention to "Uncle Mike." Placed in the drab green interview room nearby, with a few battered chairs and an institutional-style desk, Uncle Mike was again given his Miranda warning, and then signed a waiver that allowed him to speak to police, on the record, without an attorney being present representing his best interests.

"I'm not nervous that you wanted to talk to me," he told Fryman. "I'm in the process of getting my marriage back on the right track with my wife. I'll help you guys in any way possible."

Fryman sagged a bit inside. The guy sounded like he had nothing to hide, but then again, so do most killers. So the detective told him that based on his statement, they would make a determination as to whether he could continue his journey to Missouri. If he was truthful—and helpful—he'd be on his way.

"Do you know the Jones family?" Fryman asked.

"I occasionally do mechanical work along with other odds-and-ends jobs for them. When I do odd jobs for them, they occasionally would pay me with crack."

He paused for a second and then added for clarity, "Cocaine."

Joselyn was casual in the way he described the deal, and with good reason. Drug charges were minor. Besides, he carried no drugs and therefore no physical evidence. Nor would any judge allow police to admit this in a court of law, for fear of violating his Fifth Amendment right not to self-incriminate.

"Do you know someone by the name of Terrell who lives at Liz Jones's house?"

"No, I don't know him," Joselyn answered.

Like the rest of the victims, Watkins too had a record of low-level drug dealings and other misdemeanors. To refresh Joselyn's memory, Fryman showed him a mug shot of Watkins. Looking at the picture for a few moments seemed to jog his memory.

"Yes, I do know him," Joselyn said after a while. "Terrell would occasionally sell us dope. I remember someone yelling at Terrell about selling him dope and coming up short."

Jones didn't get a good "count."

"Terrell was a little off mentally," Joselyn added. "I don't see how he could be selling dope."

Not that you had to be smart to be a drug dealer.

"Did Terrell occasionally ride in your truck?" Fryman asked.

"No," Joselyn answered.

"Well, the Joneses stated that you called their residence for Terrell on several occasions."

"They're lying," Joselyn shot back. "I think they implicated me because they want to get the attention off of them."

Maybe a family member had done it. Or maybe the Jones family didn't want to be investigated for drug sales. Not a bad theory. No one likes to be questioned by police, let alone about the murder of a loved one. You didn't have to be familiar with a homicide investigation to know cops will focus first on family and friends. *NCIS* could tell you that.

Yet so far there was no evidence tying Joselyn to Watkins's murder, except that Joselyn knew him, had bought drugs from him, and drove a white truck that Jones's family saw and thought might be involved with Terrell's disappearance and murder. Fryman still had to wonder if Michael Joselyn might be their serial killer. Or maybe he was what he seemed to be—an innocent man.

"You know, I really didn't know Terrell, but I would like to know what happened to him. You guys are asking me questions about him, but you're not telling me why I'm at the police department. That makes me nervous."

Joselyn was technically not in custody. He had not been charged with a crime. He could have left at any time. Part of the detective's art is getting the subject to stay put and allow questioning without being charged. Now the detectives finally told him the truth.

"We're investigating a homicide. Terrell is dead."

Joselyn thought about that for a moment.

"I'd be willing to take a lie-detector test, because I know for a fact that I had nothing to do with the homicide," he said firmly.

"This investigation may take a couple of days," Fryman advised.

Actually, it had already been going on for eight years, but who was counting?

"Well, I'll make myself available to you guys when you need me."

He didn't appear to have anything to hide. And he told the detective that Winter's last name was Lewis. Satisfied he had gotten all he could out of Joselyn for now, Fryman released him. Now it was time to find Winter. She had allegedly been the one in the truck with Joselyn when they ran into Terrell. Fryman turned to his street contacts, who told him that Winter hung with a guy named Frank Jagger. Fryman got his address from a junkie.

As it turned out, Fryman knew Jagger, a tall, slim man from a previous case. Fryman got into his car and took off through the streets of Houma, eventually spotting Jagger. It was easy to find him; he drove a custom-made GTO. Using the siren and lights, Fryman pulled Jagger over. Fryman told Jagger he was trying to locate Winter Lewis.

According to Jagger, Winter lived at the third trailer on Matthews Drive. He had walked her there about thirty minutes before Fryman pulled him over. She was wearing a black skirt and red shirt. Fryman followed the lead and drove over to the trailer park. He knocked on the door of the third trailer, and the tenant who answered refused to give his name, which was his constitutional right.

However, the man did say that Winter Lewis was in the trailer. He then gave police, who did not have a warrant, permission to enter. Inside, Fryman and another detective found Lewis wearing the exact same clothing Joselyn had described She was handcuffed and taken into the Houma Police Department headquarters for questioning.

The cops read Lewis her rights and then presented her with a form that waived those rights, allowing police to question her without a lawyer being present. She signed it.

"Are you familiar with August Watkins?" Fryman began.

"I don't know who he is," she responded.

Just as he had done with the room's previous occupant, Fryman showed her August Watkins's mug shot.

"I know him by the nickname 'Cornbread.'"

That was a new one: "Cornbread."

"Okay, when was the last time you saw Cornbread?"

"Possibly last week or during the end of March on Matthews Drive."

As they continued to speak, Fryman was able to narrow it down further.

"The last time I saw Cornbread was April eighth."

That was the day he disappeared.

"I remember talking to him and Jack Pennington in front of the Soul Castle on Matthews Drive. As I was talking to them, I saw a green van with tan lines pull up and Jack got close to it. He was talking to the guy in the van while Cornbread stood there waiting for him."

Then, according to Lewis's statement, a friend of hers pulled up in a red car. She got in and they went to a friend's house, where Lewis stayed a while. When she was dropped off at the Soul Castle later in the day, no one was around.

"Another friend of mine was there, a little drunk dude. He wants to have a relationship with me. I asked the drunk dude [she didn't know his name] where everyone else was and he just said they had left."

The detectives confirmed her allegations, that she was with a white male who had a white truck. She also appeared to be the last one to have seen Watkins alive.

"Jack was actually the last person to be with Terrell. I don't hang out with white guys, so no one should be saying that I was seen with a white guy!"

She made it sound like to be with a white man was an insult. Perhaps to her it was.

At this point, the phrase "wild goose chase" comes to mind.

That's what Fryman and the police were tangled up in. It was almost like they were in a parallel universe—in pursuit of the phantom white truck with the phantom white guy driving, who might have picked up August Watkins that night and transported him to his death. Yet there was no physical evidence this story was true.

But the story of the phantom van was at least partially right. The person who had picked up, strangled, and dumped Terrell Watkins and other men was indeed a white guy at the wheel of a white vehicle. Though they didn't know it yet, the police had already started to solve the case.

It was time to go all the way.

CHAPTER TWELVE

THE FIRECRACKER

Lafourche, Terrebonne, and Assumption Parishes, 2005

Be careful what you wish for.

Dennis Thornton wanted a task force to take on the serial killer. He took the murders in his own parish personally. That's what made him particularly suited for his vocation. For most detectives, personal feelings were forcibly repressed. Thornton was the direct opposite: not only did he have feelings about what had happened, he also had theories.

Thornton had already surmised that the killer was mobile, picking up his victims on the street. That was the MO he had established since his early activities in New Orleans at Rawhide. The killer would transport his victims, kill them, and dump their bodies. What happened in between was anybody's guess.

Dawn Bergeron hadn't ever been on a serial-killer case, except for her experience on the periphery of this one. Then again, neither had Thornton or anybody else. Despite its media coverage, serial killing is still a very rare crime in comparison to other types of homicide. Few cops ever work such a case. Yet in Southern Louisiana, detectives in half a dozen different parishes had been chasing a deadly serial killer for eight years, through a new millennium, without any success in capturing him, before he killed and killed again and again and again.

The fact that the case had stayed out of the cable-channel news and therefore avoided the kind of media saturation that inevitably follows the story of a serial killer can be attributed to the profile of the victims. Dead black men, gay or not, doesn't sell on the news. White girls being killed by a black serial killer, on the other hand—*that* sells and gets coverage.

Up in Baton Rouge, the police had recently caught the Baton Rouge Serial Killer, a.k.a. Derrick Todd Lee. He was an African American man who killed white coeds, many from Louisiana State University. Because of his choice of victim, the state allocated the resources to capture him. If Dominique had only chosen different victims, whose lives were more valued by society, then the state might have acted earlier.

But, eventually, act they did. The numbers finally added up.

The recent spate of killings in Houma had pushed the "kill total" to fifteen, high enough to get the attention of the state's criminal justice system, where it could not be denied that there was a serial killer operating in Southern Louisiana parishes. Whoever this guy was, he seemed to thrive on raping, then strangling or suffocating all of his male victims. It fueled him.

Who it was who made the decision to form the task force isn't clear. All evidence in official records indicates that the state was simply doing its job, finally marshaling all forces available to bring in a public enemy. Unsurprisingly, Dennis Thornton was the first one to answer the summons to help.

"It was April 2005 when I got a call that Houma was having problems. They had a string of unsolved murders. The state was interested in forming a task force to track down the serial killer they thought responsible. They wanted me to join," he later recalled.

The state knew of Thornton's long investigation of the serial killer, and that he would readily agree to help. That's why he got the first call. His experience and dedication would be invaluable. There followed a big organizational meeting at state-police headquarters in Baton Rouge. Present were fourteen cops representing six parishes and the state and federal government, all invited by blue-ribbon invitation.

Besides Thornton, there was Houma parole officer Tom Lambert; Jack Erskine, an FBI agent from New Orleans; and Simon Fryman of the Houma Police Department. And of course Dawn Bergeron from Terrebonne Parish. Dawn Bergeron's boss, Major Vernon Bourgeois of the Terrebonne Parish Sheriff's Office, realized how important this task force was.

Bourgeois saw they needed the "Firecracker," Dawn Bergeron. Showing the kind of leadership that helps move the country forward by obliterating gender discrimination, Bourgeois appointed a woman as the department's lone representative on the task force. The parishes then brought in the work that they had done on the linked murder cases.

Behind the scenes, Thornton and his parish had taken the lead in working the cases in their jurisdiction and linking them with the killings in the Houma area. FBI Agent Erskine pointed out that the task force would have instant access to proprietary federal law-enforcement databases. But it would all come down to how well they could cooperate: whether they could tap into that unique chemistry that develops when smart, unbiased cops get together.

"I kind of liked not having any publicity on the case," Thornton said. "This way, we could pursue our investigation without the media being on top of our every move."

He was right. Having a talking head like Wolf Blitzer reporting on the case as though it was one big carnival would not help to solve it. Thornton still couldn't figure out how the killer seduced the victims. What about the inducements for those who weren't gay? What set him off? The questions kept going around and around in his head.

One thing Bergeron, Thornton, and the others on the task force could agree on at their first meeting was that all fifteen murders were committed by the same perpetrator. Because the serial killer was currently operating in Terrebonne Parish, the task force decided that their investigation would center on events there.

Bergeron knew her parish, knew her people well. She had been on the job long enough to appreciate what life was like for street people like the ones who had been killed. She knew about their peripatetic, pathetic lives. Unless you were someone who had been homeless, or a police officer interacting with the homeless, you had no idea what it felt like to not have a home or even hope for one. She also knew the outlying areas of the parish, where you could take a road for miles without seeing a living soul.

Regarding the deceased, Bergeron cared not one wit about their sexual orientation. To her, it was only relevant insofar as what it told her about the killer and his own sexual preferences. All of the deceased were entitled, just like anyone else, to the same efforts by the law to bring their killers to justice. Made no difference if they were gay or straight; they were *victims*.

Serendipity came into play when Thornton and Bergeron met at the first task-force conference in Baton Rouge in April 2005.

That she and Thornton would not only get along but complement each other was a stroke of luck or the divine, depending on perspective and belief. Thornton and Bergeron became the lead detectives on the case, while officers representing the cream of the crop of Louisiana law enforcement rounded out the task force.

They were acutely aware that the serial killer could strike at any moment—that time was severely limited. Both cops had the ability to do what was necessary in a serial-killer investigation to get the bad guy: think outside the box. Creative policing strategies and interviewing techniques would be crucial in bringing the perpetrator to ground. Thornton and Bergeron were particularly well suited to the job.

"We are leaving Baton Rouge," Thornton later recalls, "ready to go to work together, and Kurt Cunningham's body shows up floating in a ditch in Lafourche Parish."

Just as the state was in the process of organizing its Houma-based task force, the serial killer struck yet again.

Twenty-three-year-old Kurt Cunningham lived in Thibodaux. Unlike most of the other victims, he was white. Last seen in Houma on April 8, Cunningham's partially clad body was discovered twenty days later in a ditch off Highway 307 in Kraemer. The intervening days between death and discovery meant that Cunningham was not a "fresh kill."

While the coroner could not say for certain the cause of death was asphyxiation, he couldn't rule it out either. Thornton and Bergeron immediately suspected their serial killer had struck again. To systematize their investigation and take advantage of all their resources, the detectives developed a standard protocol on how to work the crime scene.

"The idea was that every time there was a killing, the evidence would go to the same lab, take the same path, and we'd do the same core investigative work. Working the crime scene, every member of the task force had a role," says Thornton.

And then there was thinking outside the box.

"We started experimenting, getting prints from Cunningham's skin," Thornton relates. "The lower humidity level allowed us to remove the prints. I saw this on *CSI*."

Someplace, *CSI* star and producer William L. Peterson must be smiling. His TV show was helping to solve a real-life serial-killer case! Whether it was art imitating life or the other way around made no difference. The task force was engaged in trying to put together a forensic link between the victims and their killer.

Thornton and Bergeron were deep into the Cunningham investigation when the killer struck again. This time, the victim was Alonzo Hogan. He was a twenty-eight-year-old black man, last known to reside on Highway 1 in Raceland. Hogan's body was discovered fully clothed on July 2, 2005. Had Dominique's MO changed or was this an isolated departure from the norm?

He hadn't changed his choice of dump site. True to form, the killer had dumped Hogan in a cane field in St. Charles Parish off Highway 306. Yet nothing showed up at the crime scene that could link the new victim forensically to the others. As for the autopsy, the coroner said that Hogan had been strangled and raped.

Well, that was a link, but it was frustrating not be able to establish a *direct* link. Poring over old reports, looking at new ones, re-questioning relatives of the deceased and friends for any clues, Thornton and Bergeron worked from April through August 2005, trying to discover the killer's identity. Even pooling resources, it was to no avail. Nothing worked.

Then, as if to rub their faces in it, the killer murdered yet again.

Once more it was a Houma resident, Wayne Smith. His fully clothed body was discovered on August 16 in a ditch off Grand Caillou Road. Smith's manner of death was ruled "undetermined" by the coroner. Strangling or suffocation could not be ruled out. Last known to reside on Roselawn Avenue, Smith, an African American, was all of seventeen years old, the youngest-known victim of the serial killer.

Just as with the previous murder, it was the same established autopsy protocol, the same evidence-collection protocol, and the same lack of leads. Bergeron took Thornton out into the parish so he could better get the lay of the land. They started speculating about where the killer might be living.

If they tried searching every trailer and house in the parishes, it would take them years. Obviously, they needed to narrow the field. While they had access to proprietary databases, they had very little in terms of physical hardware to use in the field. For example, the entire task force only had access to one GPS tracking unit. That meant one person dedicated to showing up at the dump site to get the proper GPS coordinates.

Much of the task force's work was going back into the past and reading the records of the old murders—trying to come up with a methodology to approach them in a new, fresh way, in hope of answers. As Bergeron recalls, they went through the records of killings in the southern part of the state, the ones that were unsolved. They needed to differentiate between the crimes their killer committed and the ones that weren't linked.

One of the things they noticed was that nearly all of the victims had been picked up on the streets. Some were gay hustlers, some were not, but they had all been raped. She checked at the gay bar in Terrebonne Parish to see if anyone remembered anything suspicious. Nothing. No one had seen or heard anything out of the ordinary.

CHAPTER THIRTEEN

RONALD J. DOMINIQUE

Assumption and Terrebonne Parishes, 2005

Though four or five victims had worn no shoes, the sheriff's conclusion that shoelessness was signature behavior turned out to be incorrect. The rest of the victims had been wearing shoes.

But in analyzing the old reports, Bergeron noticed an actual common thread: the killer had picked up three or possibly four of his victims at the Sugar Bowl Motel or close to it. It was one of his trolling grounds.

And every one of the victims had previously been convicted of at least one crime—everything from low-level misdemeanors to felonies. Then there was the Lake Houmas Inn. Bergeron knew prostitutes and drug dealers hung out there. She knew some people will do anything for a hit of crack. A "user" needs to get dope, whatever it takes. If the killer offered drugs for sex, he'd get quite a few takers.

Thornton had his own perspective.

"I looked at this in two parts," Thornton explains. "He literally put Mitchell Johnson a few feet away from LeBanks. And the FBI profiler—he had originally told us that the killer lived near the airport."

That would turn out to be right. Boutte, where Dominique lived at the time, was only miles from the airport.

"The FBI came back in 2005, when the task force was formed, in a different way. There was a different tempo. All the evidence went to the same lab, the same path, the same core investigative work at the crime scene. Everyone had a role," Thornton continued.

Cunningham and Smith had been murdered in the brief time the task force had been operative. What's more, those killings had been reported—publicly. The task force was no longer cloaked in anonymity. Results were expected both inside and outside law enforcement. The bosses wanted the case solved and the newspapers wanted a follow-up story to the killings.

Everyone was tense, hoping the next lead would be the one that closed the case.

In the task force squad room where they were working—office space donated by the sheriff of St. Charles Parish—they had charts and maps posted on the walls, with thumbtacks to literally pin down logistics. Working methodically, Thornton and Bergeron had the feeling they might be getting closer. Then Mother Nature intervened and, for a time, shut the task force down.

On August 28, 2005, Hurricane Katrina hit Louisiana, calling to mind the line from John Lennon's song "Beautiful Boy": "Life is what happens to you while you're busy making other plans."

Katrina was one of the five deadliest hurricanes in US history. A Category 3 hurricane at landfall, it hit the Gulf Coast on

August 29, 2005. In all, 1,836 people were killed. It was the cost-liest natural disaster ever to ravage the United States, with dam-ages totaling $100 billion. When the Mississippi levees gave in to the flood waters, half of New Orleans was submerged. Even Yancy Derringer—who saves New Orleans from threatening flood waters in the twentieth episode of the eponymous Desilu TV series—couldn't have done anything about it.

The city lost electricity and fresh water, becoming for a time a lawless black hole. Millions of people were homeless, fleeing on Interstate 10. Some made it down to Houma, where things were safer. The bayous had overflowed and the flood waters had taken out some houses and businesses that had the misfortune to be on the flood plains. The damage, however, was compara-tively light.

The recovery process following the storm was stymied by the federal government's strange inaction. All along the rav-aged coastline, Louisiana residents waited in vain for President George W. Bush to send in federal assistance. They were left to pick up the pieces themselves. Fortunately, picking up the pieces in Houma was easier than in New Orleans.

Once the flood waters subsided, the people of Houma assessed the damage, called their insurance companies, and went on with their lives. Thornton and Bergeron were desper-ate to jump-start the investigation before the killer struck again. They didn't have to wait long.

Chris DeVille was a forty-year-old African American who had a place on Roselawn Avenue in Houma. He wasn't the typical victim that this serial killer preferred. His family background was completely different.

Chris DeVille came from an intact family. People cared for him. His brother, in fact, had been a cop. Whether that meant another change of MO or not was hard to say. Like Alonzo Hogan, DeVille's body was fully clothed, dumped in a ditch off Highway 1 in Assumption Parish.

Meanwhile, the bosses were applying the pressure to Bergeron and Thornton. Whether in person or phone conferences, the message was clear: solve the case. They had taken long enough to establish a task force and now the higher-ups felt it was taking too much time to get a suspect in custody.

But worse for Bergeron and Thornton than this pressure was the stress they put on *themselves* to solve it.

"I was so tired by the end of it," says Bergeron.

"Dawn and I wondered about one thing that was particular. The guy seemed to pick on black males, seventeen to forty, with toned bodies. They seemed to be guys capable of taking care of themselves," Thornton adds.

They figured the killer must have immobilized them by tying them up. But why would the victims submit to *that*? Still, Thornton figured that the risk to whoever was killing was minimal. The only risk was to the victim. The killer was using instrumental violence; he had the ability to hurt, and did it in order to show his power and aggression.

Their quarry may have known about the task force, but by then it made no difference. Dominique had developed a pattern of killing that overwhelmed common reason.

John Banning, like many in Southern Louisiana, had recently served time on a minor drug offense and was on parole. His parole officer was Tom Lambert, who, by chance, was also a member of the serial-killer task force. Banning was looking to score some money. He was also pretty horny. Dominique spotted Banning walking along the highway. He drove over in the black Sonoma, pulled in in front of him, and opened the passenger-side window.

"Hey, want a beer?" Dominique yelled. "Where you going up the road?"

Banning came closer, leaning in on the passenger side, looking Dominique over. Dominique, in turn, had sized him up quickly. The selection process was hit or miss. Dominique figured this guy, correctly, for being a straight dude. That's when he whipped out the picture that he had ready to lure his straight victims.

"How'd you like to fuck this attractive white girl?" Dominique asked. "She'd really like to make it with a guy like you."

Like many men, Banning began thinking with a certain part of his anatomy below the waist. Dominique certainly didn't look dangerous. Relaxed, comfortable, and horny, Banning got in the Sonoma. Dominique drove through the parish, past the town square where the Union soldiers had met their fate, then took a left up to Bayou Blue Road, where he took a second left.

"Don't be surprised that I want to tie you up," he told Banning matter-of-factly.

What was that about? the parolee must have wondered.

"There's a stigma in the world about being gay," said Dominique out of nowhere.

How did Banning respond? Well, when Dominique pulled into his sister's driveway, he stayed. On the other side of his sister's house were the electric and water lines attached to Dominique's trailer. Feeling he needed to get away from the shipyard, he had recently gotten it towed back to his sister's house.

Then, once he and Banning were inside the trailer, Dominique began the con.

"I'll tie you up now. Take off your clothes," he told Banning.

Where was the girl he promised? Banning must have wondered. It didn't feel right; something was way off. Banning looked around and noticed the trailer was full of old clothes.

There were Christmas decorations up all over the place, though it wasn't Christmas. And there was a portable toilet. There were even what looked like jugs of urine beside it. But it was the stuff on the floor that really bothered Banning.

Stacks and stacks of gay pornography.

Banning turned to leave and Dominique didn't stop him. The trailer door clattered behind him. Banning began running toward the highway. He had the feeling that something strange had just happened, as if he had just walked over his own grave. Reaching the street, he thumbed his way back to Houma.

In such a way he became that rarity in American criminal history: a survivor of the new millennium's worst serial killer, who, as it happened, had still not been apprehended.

Thornton and Bergeron discussed it for hours. The notion that an intended victim might escape had occurred to them.

"Supposing he picks someone up he can't handle?" Thornton wondered out loud.

"And they don't want to stay, what then?" Bergeron added.

Thornton figured if the victim was already bound, the killer could kill him, probably with little resistance. But if the victim was unbound and decided he wanted to leave, then the killer would find himself in a spot. Would he just let him go? Until they found someone who'd gotten away, they could only guess.

Thornton and Bergeron had already been through the department's archives of sex offenders, with no results. However, they hadn't considered parolees as part of their investigation. Not as suspects, but witnesses. When they realized this oversight, Thornton approached parole officer Tom Lambert to inquire if it was possible to go through his client list systematically, one by one, to ask each of the parolees if they'd lately encountered anyone especially bizarre, say, or someone who insisted on bondage prior to sex. Lambert readily agreed and went back to his office. He began calling, one after another, the men on his list of fifty parolees.

When he got to John Banning, the story clicked.

"It was a few weeks ago," Banning told Lambert. "I was walking down the highway, when this guy came along in a black Sonoma truck. He was a fat white guy. He came over to talk to me and told me he could fix me up with this gorgeous white girl. He showed me a picture of her, so I got in the truck and he went off."

"Where to?"

"Bayou Blue," Banning answered.

He offered to take his parole officer out to the place. Lambert phoned Thornton and told him what he had discovered.

"We'll be right there."

Thornton grabbed his suit jacket, motioned to Bergeron to follow him, and filled her in on the way outside to their car. Once they arrived on Bayou Blue Road, they were met by Lambert and Banning in the church parking lot across from Dominique's sister's house. Banning pointed to the trailer. Cautiously, Thornton and Bergeron approached it.

Dressed in business suits, they stood out glaringly in the run-down neighborhood. Given how quiet the street was at midday, however, it was unlikely anyone noticed. Thornton opened the mailbox at the curb and Bergeron reached in. She pulled out the mail, thumbed through it for a moment, then held up an envelope.

"Ronald J. Dominique," she said with a bright smile.

PART THREE

CLOSING IN

CHAPTER FOURTEEN

SURVEILLANCE

Terrebonne Parish, November 2005

With their visit to Bayou Blue Road, Thornton, Bergeron, and the task force now (finally!) had a suspect.

But that in itself meant nothing but a suspicion. They still had to put a case together. And not just put it together, but make it airtight to guarantee a conviction. They could not run the risk of the serial killer being acquitted.

Bergeron and Thornton discussed it. How were they going to nail this guy? They decided to begin the process by bringing in the suspect—that was all Dominique was—for questioning. So far, the detectives had nothing that tied him directly to any of the murders. You need evidence for a conviction. Yes, direct evidence was best, but circumstantial evidence could also put the guy behind bars. Or in the death chamber.

Bergeron and Thornton went back to Bayou Blue Road and knocked on the trailer door. Dominique opened it. The detectives were looking at a short, portly, disheveled middle-aged man in a white T-shirt. Could this be their serial killer? Was he the man, evil personified, who had raped and killed twenty-one victims? Bergeron wondered.

Dominique's appearance certainly seemed ordinary. Not unusual. Only in movies and on TV do bad guys look especially bad. Actors who look evil are cast in evil roles. It's called typecasting, an immediate, shorthand way for directors to telegraph to the viewer who a character is.

Nevertheless, Thornton had the same suspicions as Bergeron. But like his partner, he gave no indication of them to the suspect.

"We have some questions we'd like to ask you regarding a case we are working on," Thornton informed him casually. "Would you come with us for an interview?"

This was part of the policeman's art: persuasion. Dominique was not under arrest and he didn't have to go with them. The idea wasn't to spook the guy, but rather the direct opposite. It therefore came as no surprise when Dominique responded politely.

"Sure."

Cooperating with their wishes, Dominique accompanied the two detectives to their headquarters. Inside the small, drab interview room of the Terrebonne Parish Sheriff's Office, Dominique was offered a chair. The detectives took the two seats opposite him, across a table. On the table was a tape recorder. Dominique remained very calm. Strangely enough, it was the cops who were nervous.

"It was like, 'We gotta do this.' I had never heard of anything like this before," Thornton said later. "So many murders, all of the men raped. What kind of person would do *that*?"

The detectives, who'd never tackled such a case nor sat in such close proximity to a potential serial killer—potentially the most prolific in the first decade of the new century—suppressed their feelings and forged ahead.

They followed procedure, first reading Dominique his Miranda rights, then asking him to sign forms that waived his right to have an attorney present during questioning. Dominique complied willingly with their request. He was calm, cool, collected. Thornton turned on the tape recorder.

"Okay, Mr. Dominique," Thornton began in an even voice. "We had a complaint from a John Banning. He's a parolee. He said he had been at your trailer on Bayou Blue and that you had tried to tie him up."

"I'm gay," Dominique answered quickly, perhaps too quickly. "Tying up John was just part of a sex game, nothin' more than that."

Like many serial killers, Dominique was a con man. If he were a sociopath, it would probably have been easy for him to pass a lie detector. Because serial killers don't feel guilt over the deaths they cause, their lying doesn't usually register with the machine. Even a person who did have a conscience but remained calm while connected to the machine could sometimes pass.

That's why polygraph evidence is not admissible in court. But the police had one forensic way to tie Dominique to the homicides: the recovered hairs and semen on the bodies that remained unidentified. But before the lab could test the forensic evidence, Dominique would have to consent to give them samples. Could they convince him to cooperate?

Thornton posed that request. For the first time, Dominique broke his cool.

"What's all this about?" he asked warily.

"Mr. Dominique, we're just trying to clear these cases we're working on, and so if you could help us, that would be wonderful."

Thornton stiffened, trying not to show his anxiety. He had nothing to worry about. His education and experience became a bear trap that Dominique stepped into when he nodded his consent to the procedure to get his DNA.

"I don't have anything to hide," Dominique stated.

The grammar was correct. However, the words had the ring of a lie. Time to go to the hilt.

"What we're gonna do," Bergeron continued matter-of-factly, "is ask you to sign this Consent to DNA form."

Bergeron was trying the warm approach that often put suspects at ease. Dominique looked over the form, saw nothing wrong, and signed it. He had a feral intelligence that had enabled him to escape the police those eight years, but he was still not a criminal—let alone legal—mastermind. With the form signed, the detectives summoned police technicians.

The technicians came in and took hair samples from Dominique and swabs from inside his mouth. The samples were carefully placed in evidence containers and labeled. It was important to maintain the chain of custody, so if they did get a match, a defense attorney would have difficulty challenging it in court. Now they finally had the opportunity to try their DNA tests to tie him to the murders.

The samples would be sent to the police lab. Technician Allan Barry would compare them with the evidence gathered from the victims. The hope was for a nuclear-DNA match that would nail Dominique conclusively. If, however, it came back with a positive mitochondrial match, that would still be strong circumstantial evidence, enough to file charges for murder.

After he had done his best to help the cops convict him, Dominique was thanked profusely by Thornton and Bergeron for his cooperation. They told him he was free to go and offered to give him a ride back to his trailer, which he accepted. They drove him back, dropped him off, and then reversed direction back to their office.

Now that they had a prime suspect, they brought John Banning in for questioning. He explained how Dominique had used the ruse of fucking a white girl to get him into the car. That might account for how he persuaded his straight victims into homosexual encounters.

"What would you have done if he tried to force you down?" Thornton asked.

"Brother, it would have been like Pearl Harbor!" Banning answered succinctly.

After Banning was dismissed, Thornton had another idea.

"Let's go back into the database."

Bergeron nodded.

"Maybe there was something that was overlooked."

They began by opening the database of sex offenders.

"Let's make sure we cover the guys who were charged, but not convicted," said Thornton.

Surprise, surprise. Dominique had a record after all. Up came the old rape charge in Thibodaux Parish from the late 1990s. On August 25, 1996, Dominique was arrested for committing forcible rape and held on a $100,000 bond.

"According to neighbors, a partially dressed young man escaped from the window of Dominique's home in Thibodaux, screaming that he had tried to kill him. When the case was brought to court, the victim could not be found to testify. In November 1996, the judge continued the case indefinitely."

It was similar to what had happened with Banning.

"He wasn't convicted," Thornton said over Bergeron's shoulder.

And there was more. They found the 2002 assault he had been involved in.

On February 10, 2002, Ronald J. Dominique screamed at a woman who, he said, had hit a baby stroller with her car. This was in a parking lot at a Mardi Gras parade in Terrebonne Parish. Allegedly, the woman apologized, but to Dominique, the picture of righteousness, that wasn't enough. So he kept screaming at her until, finally, he slapped her face. Once more he was offered a deal.

Dominique agreed to go into a parish alternative-sentencing program in lieu of trial. In October 2002, he was released from the program, having met all conditions of his deal. It was because of Dominique's court problems during that period of time that he did not troll and kill. He was too busy satisfying the conditions of his deal on the lesser charge.

Two years earlier, in 2000, Dominique had gotten a ticket for disturbing the peace. He'd pled guilty and paid a fine. But things didn't stop there. The detectives found that on May 15, 1994, Dominique got busted for drunken driving. And going back nine years before that, on June 12, 1985, they discovered his arrest for making the dirty phone calls, for which he pled guilty, paying the fine and court costs.

There were also two more rape charges: Dominique had been accused of sodomizing two men. Both charges were later dropped.

"Let's see what happened," said Thornton.

The charges were in Thibodaux Parish, so Bergeron called the Thibodaux Parish Sheriff's Office. Speaking to detectives there, she explained that they were part of the task force working on the Southern Louisiana serial-killer case. Without telling them what she had already found out, she asked, "Could you go through every sex offender in the parish and see if Ronald J. Dominique comes up for raping men?"

Keeping Bergeron on the line, the Thibodaux detectives looked, but couldn't find anything. Dubious as to their conclusion, Bergeron drove over to the Thibodaux Parish Sheriff's Office and personally went through the sex-offender files herself. When she returned to Terrebonne, she held two files in her hands.

"Those guys claimed they couldn't find anything on Dominique," she said, a trifle sarcastically.

They had apparently misplaced or just failed to find the files, which she handed to Thornton.

"The charges were dropped for lack of corroborating evidence," she continued.

Thornton called the investigating officer on both cases, Sam Alper, who was, to say the least, *surprised* that Dominique was their serial-killer suspect. He remembered him all right.

"He had this persecution complex about being gay. He said that being gay left him open to ridicule."

Despite the fact that both detectives felt they were closing in, they were forced to go slowly. There wasn't enough evidence to convince the higher-ups to commit the monetary resources to surveil Dominique full-time. They could, and did, have squad cars go by his trailer, but they couldn't keep track of him 24–7.

Still, Thornton and Bergeron knew they had the right guy. They needed to stop him before he murdered again.

Going back over the old reports of the killer's murders, Thornton and Bergeron saw that at least three of the victims had been picked up near the Sugar Bowl Motel on Highway 182. Locals called it New Orleans Boulevard.

"Let's put a roadblock out there. It might slow him down and give him some pause," Bergeron suggested to her partner.

Thornton agreed. The detectives requested that a roadblock be put up on New Orleans Boulevard until the case was finished. Cars would be regularly stopped and searched for anything suspicious. If they were right about it being one of the killer's trolling grounds, they had just it cut off.

It was a good idea, but it didn't take into consideration the killer's ingenuity. While they had, indeed, cut off one of his trolling grounds, he could simply find another to replace it. Dominique was intimately familiar with Houma's unique landscape.

Nick Pellegrin was a young hustler who needed money.

On November 5, 2005, he was working on his house when the meter reader arrived. Pellegrin noticed he was sort of heavy—strikingly so, given his short height.

"How you doing?" asked Dominique brightly.

Pellegrin answered that he was fine, just doing some work on his house.

"Hey, how about I come by later, after work, and we go and have some fun?"

A proposition of sex for money, as old as the Bible.

Pellegrin who was twenty-one years old and white, needed the money. He readily agreed but had to finish the job he was doing. Could Dominique come back when he was finished? Promising to do just that, Dominique returned hours later and picked him up. Dominique then drove to his sister's house. As dusk was just beginning to settle in, he opened the door of his trailer.

Nick Pellegrin entered into hell.

CHAPTER FIFTEEN

GETTING THE GOODS

Lafourche and Thibodaux Parishes,
November 2005–December 2006

This time, Dominique had to be much more careful not to allow his victim to scream. Before, his trailer had been in an empty field where no one could hear him kill. Here, with the trailer parked next to his sister's house, not only she would hear the sound, but also anyone else around, including the churchgoers right across the street.

Four days later, Pellegrin's fully clothed body was discovered in a wooded area in Lafourche Parish. There were ligature marks on his wrists; Bergeron and Thornton were summoned. When they arrived at the dump site, they were royally pissed off. The killer had slipped right through their roadblock.

The two detectives attended the autopsy, in which the coroner determined the manner of death was homicide due to strangulation. There was a scalp laceration at the back of the head and ligature marks on the wrists.

"Maybe he knocked the guy out before he killed him," Thornton posited. "That would account for the head laceration."

"That makes sense," his partner answered, "especially since some of the other victims have those injuries."

Thornton still had no answers, just the bare facts. Nick Pellegrin had been strangled and raped. That was consistent with the previous twenty-one murders. Pellegrin was victim number twenty-two. The two detectives went to notify his next of kin.

After that, with their duty done, they went back to the sheriff's office where they discussed bringing Dominique in immediately. The problem was a lack of evidence, any evidence, either direct or circumstantial. The results of the DNA testing on Dominique had not come in yet., Because it's highly skilled and sensitive work to go into the building blocks of human genetics and match them up, DNA testing can take months. The only thing they could do was wait.

When the results came in days later, it was Thornton who took the phone call. He listened, said a few words, nodded, and smiled. Then he hung up the phone.

"Remember those Caucasian chest hairs on Oliver LeBanks?" said Thornton.

"I remember reading about them," Bergeron answered.

"We got a positive match for Dominique's DNA. But it's a mitochondrial match."

They both knew what that meant. Without the nuclear DNA match, it could just as easily be someone in Dominique's family. Charging was easy; conviction was hard. They needed more to convince a jury beyond reasonable doubt. The good news was that they had enough evidence on Dominique to commit additional resources to the chase.

A 24–7 surveillance unit was set up immediately. In the parking lot of the church across the street from Dominique's trailer, the Feds had a huge van outfitted with eavesdropping and taping equipment, as well as night scopes. They even employed a helicopter to pass over the trailer to take pictures from the air and track Dominique if he left.

Church parishioners obviously knew something was going on.

"It was really strange," said one Bayou Blue parishioner, who just happened to worship there. "We knew something was up, but had no idea what it was."

How could anyone not know something was up, including Dominique, when the police presence was so obvious? The killer knew the detectives were on to him. For Dominique, it had been a challenge to kill at his sister's house without her knowing, and then dispose of the body by passing silent and undiscovered through the increased police presence on Houma's streets.

That after being questioned by the police! Now the net was tighter. Should he plan an escape or stay put? Rattled, he wasn't sure which way to go.

Meanwhile, Bergeron and Thornton established a timeline that matched up all twenty-two victims to Dominique's movements, residences, and jobs. They knew where he lived and worked when the men were killed. They discovered that Ronald J. Dominique was always living and working near to where the victims had disappeared.

The more they looked at the timeline, the more it fueled their conviction that they had the right guy. But they needed more facts, not to mention evidence to make the charges stick. If Dominique were tried and acquitted for lack of evidence, the double-jeopardy clause in the Constitution might prevent trying him again.

For his part, Dominique had not been up to the police pressure. He stopped cold until he could figure a way to kill undetected. During the summer of 2006, the task force continued its investigation unabated.

"We were sitting on Oliver LeBanks's mitochondrial DNA," Thornton explains. "Then we got another DNA hit, this time on Angel Mejia."

Mejia had been the eighth victim, murdered in 1999.

"Dominique had left some of his semen in Mejia's rectum," Thornton remembers. "At least we thought it was his. It wasn't nuclear but it was mitochondrial. We knew there was a connection."

But again, a mitochondrial-DNA match could have meant Dominique or anyone in his family. They decided to keep watching him. Task-force funds were limited, but they needed to surveil him 24–7 to stop him from killing again while they built their case.

"We surveilled him on our own time," says Bergeron. "It took us away from our families, our regular responsibilities. We missed weddings, graduations, other family events because we just wanted to get him. Many times, we would be working with only a few hours' sleep."

And the higher-ups expected results. The police had spent a lot of time shadowing Dominique and still there were cracks in the wall. One day, Dominique noticed a police car in the rearview mirror of his Sonoma. With a few sharp turns, he shook the tail, leaving him free, once again, to kill.

Christopher Sutterfield was last known to reside on St. Charles Bypass Road in Thibodaux Parish, Dominique's old killing grounds. A twenty-seven-year-old white male, Sutterfield had been visiting some friends in Houma when he disappeared on

October 15, 2006. The next time anyone saw him, he was dead. This time, it was a "fresh kill"—that is, the body was discovered shortly after death.

Sutterfield was dumped off Highway 69 in Iberville Parish. Dominique had really gone farther out this time to do his dumping. The task force was contacted. Bergeron and Thornton drove out to the dump site, where they encountered Sutterfield's fully clothed body. Immediately, they looked for and saw the ligature marks.

Dammit, it was Dominique again!

He'd slipped his tail. Twice he had killed while he was the prime suspect, and he knew it. Thornton and Bergeron took it personally. Neither said a word between them because each knew what the other was thinking: this would be the last time Dominique killed.

Thornton and Bergeron attended the autopsy, where the coroner said that Sutterfield's manner of death was "asphyxiation by strangulation after the victim's clothes were removed." The coroner noted redness and swelling of the rectum. Sutterfield had been raped.

Hoping Dominique might have once again ejaculated inside his victim, the coroner took swabs from Sutterfield's rectum. The evidence was rushed to the police laboratory. Meanwhile, Bergeron was scheduled to go on vacation with her daughter to Walt Disney World.

"What do you think, Dennis? Should I go?" Bergeron asked doubtfully.

They had all been going nonstop on the case. Thornton knew that Bergeron needed a break as much as he did. And he also knew she needed the time with her daughter. They all needed time with their families.

"Go on," he said. "I'll let you know if we get anything."

But Bergeron couldn't completely leave her job behind. Despite the fun-loving image she put on for her daughter, the entire time they were at Disney World, she couldn't get the killer and his victims out of her mind.

Bergeron was in her hotel room in Florida when the phone rang. It was Thornton. He had gotten the DNA results back on Sutterfield.

"There was no match on Sutterfield," Thornton said with obvious disappointment in his voice.

Bergeron said nothing. She, too, had hoped for a match. But this didn't mean it wasn't Dominique, just that in Sutterfield's case, he had left nothing behind to positively identify himself. They were still convinced that Dominique had already killed twice while the police were actively investigating and observing him.

"Really, what choice do we have? We gotta pick him up."

Bergeron agreed. Even if the charges didn't stick, right now was the time to take him into custody. Dennis Thornton approached a judge in Jefferson Parish and asked for two first-degree-murder warrants on Ronald J. Dominique. The first was for the murder of Oliver LeBanks in October 1998. The second was for the murder of Manuel Reed in May 1999. LeBanks was their best bet because of the DNA match.

Dominique, meanwhile, was running into problems with his family. His sister had grown tired of the constant surveillance and didn't want problems with the police. At loose ends, Dominique settled in a flophouse used by local oil-rig workers. He wasn't sure what was going to happen next.

Meanwhile, Thornton and Bergeron thought they were rolling the dice by arresting Dominique without an airtight case.

"It was December 2, 2006," Thornton remembers. "All we had was the mitochondrial-DNA match. There had been lots of pressure to arrest him. We knew that once we got in the inter-view room, it was anybody's guess what he might say. To make matters worse, there had been a media leakage."

No one knew how, but local reporters had found out about the impending arrest of the serial killer in their midst. When Bergeron and Thornton got out of their car at the flophouse—Dominique's sister had kindly directed them to her brother's present location—reporters crowded around them with cam-eras, microphones, lights, and pads, shouting questions which, of course, they ignored.

The last thing they needed was a defense lawyer to say they were polluting the jury pool with pejorative statements about their client.

Inside the flophouse, they found Dominique sitting pen-sively in his room. They approached him, both detectives feel-ing for the weapons at their waists in case they needed them. By prearranged plan, Thornton was to take the lead. After so many years of tracking the serial killer without knowing who he was, Thornton would now have the honor of the collar.

"Ronald J. Dominique?" Thornton asked.

His voice was strong and confident.

Dominique nodded.

"We have two warrants for your arrest on first-degree-murder charges. Please stand up."

Bergeron guided him to the wall, patted him down, and handcuffed him. With Bergeron holding his right elbow and Thornton his left, they marched Dominique outside, into the glare of the TV lights. Pushing through the crowd, the detec-tives placed him in the back of their car. Bergeron got in the back with him and Thornton drove.

"You know us from the last time we spoke, don't you, Mr. Dominique?" said Thornton.

Dominique looked at the two cops.

"Yes, I recognize you," Dominique said quietly.

When they got to the police station, they hustled him up the concrete steps into a large outside corridor that was filled with cops and reporters. Inside the station, they took their suspect past the county assessor's office. Dominique was led into a drab blue room where the interview would take place. He saw the three chairs and an institutional desk with a glass wall behind it.

Unlike on television, most police interview rooms do not have two-way glass, but this one did. Any cops who were interested in the proceedings were permitted to observe. Strangely, many of the detectives on the task force did not want the responsibility of interviewing Dominique. The gruesomeness of his crimes made even seasoned pros cringe. Bergeron and Thornton were different.

Getting him had become their mission. However, they were not going to let their personal feelings interfere with Dominique being questioned fairly. Although they were convinced of his guilt, they still had to prove it, ideally through a detailed confession.

CHAPTER SIXTEEN

BLACK PEPPER

The detectives had already decided in advance that Thornton would take the lead, being the more experienced of the two.

Seated in the interrogation room next to Bergeron, he looked across at Dominique. Thornton had done his research and knew that, if approached informally, serial killers sometimes open up in surprising ways. So he began to chat with Dominique, to gain his confidence.

After a few minutes, Dominique began talking to them about the two men whose murders he was being charged with. Perhaps he was bragging, perhaps he was happy the chase was over, or perhaps it was just that he enjoyed finally talking to people who wanted to listen to him. Whatever the reason, the detectives quickly read him his Miranda rights.

Once again, they got him to sign off on the waiver of his constitutional rights, allowing them to speak with him without a lawyer being present. If at any time he requested one, they would have to stop. On the table was a tape recorder. Thornton pushed the "on" switch.

"The following is a tape-recorded voluntary statement given by Ronald J. Dominique. The date of the statement is December 1, 2005. It's now 6:32 p.m. Present for the statement is Lieutenant Dawn Bergeron with the Terrebonne Parish Sheriff's Office and Lieutenant Dennis Thornton with the Jefferson Parish Sheriff's Office."

Thornton looked over at Dominique.

"For the record, could you state your full name please?"

"Ronald Joseph Dominique," he said in a soft voice.

"Okay, Ronald," Thornton continued, "at this time, you're willing to give us information on what you know about what happened between yourself and these two men, is that correct?"

"Yes."

The idea was to get him to confess to the two murders in the warrants. If they could do that, then they had him in jail for life. If Dominique then confessed to all twenty-three, Bergeron and Thornton would succeed in not only helping to give closure to the families involved, but also bringing to ground one of the worst serial killers in American criminal history.

With his "kill total" up to twenty-three, only five serial killers in the United States were worse: Juan Corona, who killed twenty-five ranch laborers; Wayne Williams, whose victim count reached twenty-four; John Wayne Gacy, who murdered thirty-three boys and men; Ted Bundy, known to have murdered thirty-five women; and Gary Ridgeway, who was convicted of forty-nine murders but confessed to many more.

"Let's start with the first man, Ronald. You indicated to us earlier, before we activated this tape, that you had met this man. Tell us about it."

"I met him in New Orleans and he wanted to fool around."

"Can you remember how long ago it was, Ronald?"

"I don't remember."

"Where were you living at the time?" Bergeron asked.

"I was living in Boutte," Dominique answered.

"How long did you live there?"

"Sometime after I got out of jail, maybe six months or a little longer."

Thornton got to the heart of the case.

"Now, where were you when you met the first man?"

"In the quarters. I had just started going to get out of the house. I had went maybe two or three times."

"How did you meet this guy, Ronald, in the French Quarter?"

"You just walk up and down the streets in a bar and people approach you."

"Okay and he approached you?" Thornton continued.

"Yes," said Dominique.

"What was said?"

"He wanted to know if I wanted to have a good time. I said, 'Sure.'"

"You mean sex?" Thornton asked, seemingly innocent.

"Yes."

"He approached you and asked if you wanted to fool around and have sex?" Thornton summed it up.

"Yes," Dominique answered, adding a little defensively, "That goes on all over New Orleans."

"Were you looking to have a good time?"

"I was just walking around, just enjoying the music and talking to people."

One heck of a good time, guy, Bergeron thought, remaining silent while her partner continued to work the suspect.

"I was drinking. Beer, draft beer. I had more than a couple of drinks."

"Okay, now you meet him and he starts talking first and he starts talking about having a good time, correct?"

"Yes."

"Alright, what happens next?"

Both detectives were nervous because this was the crucial point. They needed him to confess to the killing.

"We went to my vehicle, 'cause I had really not much money," Dominique continued. "I ain't had no money for no motel or nothing and he didn't have none, so we went to my vehicle. It was parked near the lakefront, riverfront, whatever. Near the Jax Brewery."

"Now what happens when you get to the car?"

"We got in," said Dominique, as casually as he was describing the weather, "and we started pulling our clothes down to our knees, past our knees, and then we started sucking on each other and doing things. In the back seat."

This guy has a good memory, Thornton thought. *We can use that to our advantage.*

"Is any part of your clothing off?" Bergeron wondered out loud.

"I have my drawers and my pants pulled down."

Drawers? He was using an antiquated, almost genteel expression for underwear.

"I pulled my shirt over my head where it was on my shoulder."

"And what about him?" Thornton asked.

"I think he took his off."

"All the way?" Thornton shot back.

"No," Dominique muttered.

"Then what happened?"

"And then he laid on his stomach and then I put my thing in him and we fooled around, and then after, he wanted to lay on me and he laid on me, and then he pulled a knife."

A knife, both of the detectives thought. *That's a new one.*

There had been no indication at any point that a knife was involved in any of the murders. None had been recovered.

"He pulled a knife out and told me that he was gonna fuck me and he wanted my money and if I didn't give it to him he was gonna kill me," Dominique insisted.

According to the law, the murder would not be premeditated if Dominique really felt his life was in danger. If a jury bought that, it was possible he'd go free.

"Okay," said Thornton carefully.

Wanting clarification, Bergeron asked, "You got on top of him and you fooled around with him. What does that mean, Ronald?"

"I put my thing in him," he answered succinctly.

That contradicted what he had just said about the victim— that he fucked him at knife point.

"And you had sex with him?"

"Yes, ma'am."

Dominique was nothing if not polite.

"Did you ejaculate?"

"Yes, ma'am."

"When you finished, what happened after that?"

"Then he got on top of me and he was just supposed to rub his thing on me 'cause I told him that I was hurt before. I was split."

Thornton glanced at Bergeron. He could see she was wondering the same thing.

"Let's talk a little bit about that, Ronald. What do you mean by you were hurt before and you were split?"

"I had a cut inside my rectum when I worked offshore. They had to cut all the infection out when I came in and stitch it."

"And how did you get that infection?" Bergeron asked.

"It was from when I messed around with this guy before I went offshore. Or it could have been the black pepper that built up when I was offshore. I started bleeding, getting pale, and my gums were raw. I had to come in for surgery."

Both detectives knew there was no known case on medical record in which a man's rectum was split open by ingesting too much black pepper. It sounded bizarre, but then again, the whole case was bizarre. Thornton forged on.

"So, it's possible," Thornton asked, "that what happened to you when you were thinking about what was going on at this time, with this guy, you were reminded of what happened in the past, about the fact you couldn't have somebody anally penetrate you?"

"Yeah," Dominique answered.

"Another man could not put his penis in your rectum? Is that fair to say?"

"Yes, 'cause when I had the surgery, it was like seven and a half weeks to recuperate 'cause I was hurt so bad."

It didn't make sense. Thornton needed him to get more specific.

"When you had this emergency, you were already working offshore and it's from, you said, a black pepper build-up or . . ."

"A guy I had sex with," Dominique said, finishing the sentence.

"This was when he anally penetrated you?"

"Uh-huh. That was the first time I ever did it."

That would mean the first time he had anal sex with a man. Dominique was in his early thirties.

"What did the doctors tell you when you healed? Did they say you shouldn't have sex anymore?" Bergeron asked.

"They told me I would be tighter and that I have to take stool softeners for the stool to come out, so I don't tear inside. If I have any problems, I was supposed to take stool softeners so it won't rip me open."

"All right, so you've had anal sex?"

"Yes," he answered.

"You were through and you ejaculated inside of him?" she continued.

"Yes. He was gonna fuck and kill me if I didn't give him no more money 'cause he had a knife by my throat."

Dominique was calm as he spoke, not even breaking a sweat.

"Now he lays you down on the seat and what did he say to you?" Thornton asked again.

"He told me he was gonna fuck me and he wanted all my money or he was gonna kill me."

Once again, Dominique was raising the specter of self-defense.

"But to get you to lay on the seat, you did that voluntarily or did he do something else?"

Thornton had caught him in the lie. All Dominique could do was answer defensively.

"I didn't think he was gonna stick it in. He said he's just gonna rub it. Then he put the knife to my throat and I gave him all the money I had, twenty dollars. He kept telling me I was lying, that I had more."

Neither cop believed him. There just wasn't the ring of truth to what he said. Maybe Dominique really was trying to set up a self-defense scenario.

"What did you do then?" Thornton asked.

"I panicked and I grabbed a tire thing and I swung it back and he fell on top of me."

"Where'd you hit him?"

"I don't know. I just jumped on top of him and I don't remember when I was choking him and he wasn't breathing."

Now, Thornton and Bergeron knew how he had immobilized LeBanks: by hitting him with a tire iron. But the choking—had he used anything to do that, or just his hands?

"What were you choking him with, Ronald?" Thornton casually asked.

"The seat belt."

"How'd you get it around his neck?" said Bergeron.

"I just pulled it around and next thing I know, he wasn't breathing."

Dominique had pulled it tight, preventing Reed from doing anything but grasping at his neck, trying to stop the belt from biting into his flesh and cutting off his air supply. Thornton had him on a roll and pushed forward.

"How did you keep him down, what did you do?"

This was a key point. Most of the victims were in good shape. Why hadn't they fought back?

"I was on top of him, his head facing the seat."

So his body weight was on top of the victim, Thornton thought.

"Is he saying anything at this point?" Bergeron asked.

"I couldn't hear nothing. I was scared."

"Could you feel him squirming?" Thornton asked.

"Yes. I held the seat belt around his neck until I noticed he wasn't breathing. Then I let it go."

Both cops had taken confessions from suspects before, but never like this, *never*.

There was little emotion in Dominique's voice. But he had what seemed like an incredible memory for detail. That's what would make the murder charges stick: the details of the murders that only the killer would know.

"Now when you stopped, what did you do then?" continued Thornton, keeping the excitement he was feeling out of his voice.

"I panicked. I was scared that if I went to the cops, they'd put me in jail because he was dead."

"You're pretty sure he was dead, right?"

"He wasn't breathing," Dominique answered.

"So you got back in the front seat of your car and drove where?" Thornton continued.

"I drove off and I just drove and drove. It looked like it was forever. All I remember is streets and lights."

Thornton remembered that the victim had been found in a dumpster.

"Tell us about the dumpster where you put him. How'd you pick it?"

Dominique couldn't remember where the dumpster was, or its location. It was simply there and convenient.

"I took him out of the car and put him in the dumpster. Then I left."

Dominique had told them enough to reveal that he had, indeed, killed LeBanks. Only someone with intimate knowledge of the crime—the killer—would have had the details that Dominique had. He had a terrific memory despite his protestations that he couldn't remember things.

"How did you take him out of the car?" Thornton continued.

"I had to grab him by his pants and grab him by the throat and just kind of pick him up and put him in."

"Now after you put him in the dumpster, what happened next?" Thornton asked.

"I drove home and turned the shower on and I just laid in the tub and cried until I fell asleep."

"Did you notice that anything that belonged to him was still in your car?" Bergeron asked.

Serial killers usually like to keep souvenirs of their victims and kills. For example, Jeffrey Dahmer took this to the hilt by keeping his victims' flesh and bones.

"No," Dominique answered.

"Okay, let's talk a little bit more about this other guy," said Thornton.

He showed him a picture of Manuel Reed.

"What can you tell me about that one?"

"I came out the bar and he wanted to fool around. We went to my car, got in the back seat like I did with the other guy. We fooled around and then when I lay down, he got me to lay on my stomach and he held me and he put it in me and started hurting me."

Hurting him?!

Dominique was talking like he was the victim. Neither detective believed him, though they put on their most sympathetic expressions.

"You're talking about this guy placing his penis in your rectum?" Thornton asked.

"Yes. I met him in a bar, I don't remember which one, and he said, 'You wanna have fun?'"

"What did you tell him, Ronald?"

"I told him yes, but I didn't have much money. I told him about my operation and he said that was fine."

"Well let me ask you this, Ronald, when you talked about your operation to this guy, did he really understand you?"

"He understood that I can't take it in the rectum."

"He was good with that?"

"Yes. He told me that he's used to letting people put it in him. In other words, doing blow jobs and letting people screw him, put their thing in his rectum."

"What about the money, you talk about that?" Bergeron asked.

"I told him I don't carry that much money, maybe twenty or thirty dollars, and he said twenty bucks is fine 'cause he just needed a little money to do something. To get some food."

"What happens when you get to your car?" asked Thornton.

"I unlock the doors, we both got in. We both pulled down our pants. First, he went down on me and then I went down on him. He gave me a blow job and then he laid on his stomach and then I put my thing in his rectum."

Thornton looked down at the tape recorder. He could see that they were almost at the end of the first side of the cassette.

"Alright, Ronald, I hate to stop you, we're gonna stop now and flip the tape over. It's now 7:02 p.m. End of first statement."

The two cops excused themselves and went outside to get him a snack.

"He offered no resistance in talking to us," Thornton recalled later. "If he wanted food, he got food, if he wanted a bathroom break, he got one. We wanted to get his full story. He's not going to be able to recount nine years in just one session in one room. But it was important to keep him talking until we got the facts on the first two murders he was initially being charged with."

After that first statement, there was only a one-minute pause to flip the tape over, and then Thornton continued.

"Okay, we're continuing now on an additional side of this statement, in our interview with Ronald J. Dominique. The time is now 7:03 p.m. Now, Ronald, you were continuing again with what happened in your car. Did he tell you his name?"

"If he did, I don't remember."

"How about the guy that ended up in the dumpster? Did he say anything about his name at all?" Bergeron asked.

"No, I don't remember. That's the first time I seen him."

"Do you ask names or does it matter to you?" Thornton asked.

"I don't remember a lot of people's names at work. I gotta ask them a bunch of times."

"But he might've told you his name?"

"Might've."

"Would you have told him your real name?"

"I always say to people, 'Call me Ron.'"

They're going to call him a serial killer now.

Bergeron listened as her partner once again got Dominique to describe fooling around with Reed before it got deadly.

"After I came, he told me to lay on my stomach and he just wanted to rub his thing on my butt. That's when he grabbed me by my shoulders and my back and he slipped it in and started screwing me. I panicked 'cause it was hurting and I grabbed the tire tool and I hit him.

"When he fell, I tried to tie his hands so he wouldn't hurt me no more. He pulled loose and I grabbed a rope I had in the back and started choking him. And I noticed he wasn't breathing no more."

"Okay, now this rope you had, where'd you keep it, Ronald?" Thornton asked.

"It was a rope I kept in the back seat of my station wagon, where it's flat."

"You're on your stomach on the back seat and you've agreed to let him get on top of you?"

"Yeah, just to rub his thing on my butt."

"Okay, now, at this point, you have already ejaculated in his rectum, is that correct?" said Thornton.

"Yes," Dominique responded.

"Where'd you hit him at?"

"I don't know, I just hit him and then when he fell, I just hurry up and grabbed the rope and had started tying his hands. And then he started coming to and started pulling and he got his hands free."

Even with his skull pounded in, Reed was fighting for his life.

"At this point you had a rope out and were tying his wrists?" asked Thornton.

"Yes, behind him."

"He's face down with his hands behind his back and you're tying his wrists?"

"Yes."

"How thick was the rope?" Bergeron asked.

"Maybe a little bit thicker than a pencil."

"How long was it?" Thornton asked.

"Maybe ten or eleven foot, maybe," the killer answered.

Whether it was the rope or the jack handle, he was prepared to immobilize and then kill his victim. That would make it premeditated murder, which in Louisiana was punishable by the death penalty.

"How long did you have to hold that rope around his neck?" Thornton asked.

"I don't remember, I was scared. I don't remember! I just kept holding it and holding it."

"What did you do after he stopped breathing?"

"I got out in front and drove somewhere where it was dark so I can get rid of him and go home. I drove somewhere where they had an overpass and it was dark. I just turned my lights off, drove in, pulled him out, and drove off."

Thornton needed him to get more specific, so he went back and ask Dominique where he dumped LeBanks's body.

"Tell me, where was this?"

"Toward Kenner."

"Remember any buildings or businesses nearby?" Thornton continued.

"No, it was dark. It looked like they had a cement wall for a overpass, but everything else was dark."

Dominique dropped off LeBanks like so much detritus and drove away.

"Ronald, see if you can remember this," said Thornton. "When you took this person out of your car, did you back out or could you completely keep going? If it's an overpass, you can go through it."

"I don't remember, it's been a long time. All I remember is I hurry up and grabbed him and pulled him out and then took off."

"How did you find this place, Ronald?"

"I don't know, I was just driving."

"Is it somewhere you had been before, somewhere you knew about?" Bergeron asked.

"No, I just drove down that street."

While he planned out in advance how he would immobilize and kill his victim, he did not seem to have any plan in particular as to the dump sites. According to Dominique, it was all improvisation.

"Now, Ronald, this particular person we're talking about here in the second photograph," said Thornton, showing him a shot of the Reed dump site, "what happened here?"

"We were just supposed to give each other head," Dominique said defensively, "and he told me I could put my thing in him, that I was gonna pay him. He was just gonna go. He just needed a little money to get him some food."

"But it didn't happen like that, did it?" said Thornton.

"No."

"Alright now, would you say when you were laying on your stomach and he put his penis in, did you want him to do that?"

"No, I told him I couldn't. He told me he was just gonna rub it on my butt."

Dominique was trying to establish a justification for killing. Thornton knew that. His job was to undermine any alibi the killer came up with.

"Would you say that he had this type of sex with you against your will?" Thornton continued.

"Yes."

"Did you tell him to stop?"

"I started screaming and told him no! He kept on."

"He kept on and that's when you used this tire tool?"

"I twisted my body and grabbed it and hit him and he fell against the back seat and me. That's when I got on top of him."

"Now let me ask you this, Ronald. We're here today, Lieutenant Bergeron and myself, to tell you that this person that you're talking about, where you had to incapacitate him and he ultimately died, you placed in a dumpster. And the first one you spoke about, you placed him under an overpass. Do you have any idea what the time difference was in those two?"

"No, sir."

"After the second one, how did you feel about going out?"

"I was just going out to get a drink. Just to get things off my mind."

Thornton looked down at the cassette. The tape was nearly to the end.

"Everything you are telling us here is truthful to the best of your knowledge?"

"Yes, sir."

"Did you give this statement of your own free will?"

"Yes, sir."

"The statement is now ended. It's the first of December, 2006, 7:19 p.m. December 1, 2006."

The tape recorder was turned off.

Bergeron and Thornton left Dominique alone in the interview room with a drink and a sandwich, and they went outside to confer.

The detectives were on *spilkes*, meaning "on edge." Their insides churned. Finally, *finally*, they were going to solve this case. And their superiors knew it: they'd been watching through the two-way glass.

Two of the twenty-three murders had now been cleared. They had Dominique where they wanted him, but with a long way to go. They had been tracking the serial killer across two millennia and they almost had him.

"Let's keep going," said Thornton.

Bergeron nodded. The iron was hot—time to strike.

CHAPTER SEVENTEEN

CONFESSION

Before they went back into the interview room, Thornton and Bergeron received a preliminary report from the crime-scene technicians.

They had towed in both of Dominique's trailers for a detailed search. The preliminary results were that Dominique had kept no souvenirs of his "kills." Or maybe he did and they just had not found them yet. The detectives went back into the interview room a few minutes later. The plan was to move from one murder to the next, and see what Dominique said about each.

Whether Dominique would give the details necessary to solve the other twenty-one cases was hard to say. When they went back into the interview room, Thornton went with the sympathetic approach again to prime him.

"I know you're suffering," said Thornton, "but we need to know, and I think you've picked this up, that there's others, Ronald. And without bringing out any more photographs, without writing anything else, if you're hearing me okay now . . ."

Bergeron turned on the tape recorder as Thornton continued to talk.

"And I know you are," Thornton continued, "and we could certainly deal with this. I think you'll agree there are others. Am I right in saying that?"

"Most probably. I just don't remember," said Dominique, trying to stall.

"Okay, 'probably.' That's fair enough that there was one more time."

"I said most probably. I just don't remember."

"Most probably," Thornton repeated. "But you just don't remember. Okay, well, that's fair enough."

"All I ask is y'all just to tell my sister, I'm not the same after I got out of jail, especially after I got raped, and I didn't mean to hurt my family."

"You're gonna get to call her if you want," Bergeron offered.

"No!"

"Okay," she replied, a little surprised at the vehemence of his reply.

She had picked up on Thornton's softer approach and was going with it herself.

"Do you wanna call?" asked Thornton sympathetically.

"I didn't mean to hurt my godchild and my sister and all! When I go in front of the judge, I'm gonna tell him just take my life."

They didn't believe him, but they didn't let on. Serial killers as a rule did not offer their own lives in place of their victims. It would have been impossible to believe that, given that Dominique had brutally raped and murdered twenty-three human beings. Proving it was another matter.

"Do you wanna talk to her?" Thornton repeated sympathetically.

"No!"

"We'll talk to her for you. What do you want us to tell her again?"

Dominique hung his head and was silent, like a schoolkid who was just caught doing something wrong. Except it was much more serious than that.

"You want to write her a note?" Bergeron suggested. "You just want us to tell her that?"

"We'll deliver whatever you want," Thornton added.

"She's the only one in the family treated me nice. Everybody else treated me like crap because I'm gay."

"I know—we know that, Ronald," said Thornton reassuringly.

It was important to keep him cooperative.

"My mother should've seen I needed help when I got out of jail but . . ."

Thornton thought about that one and how to respond. Sometimes you just wing it.

"Right. Well, look, you've had a rough life," Thornton said. "I mean you told us your family had picked on you, right? Isn't that true? And listen, we know just like what you told us with the other people."

"I didn't mean to hurt nobody."

Thornton was playing right into Dominique's paranoid self-pity act, or whatever it was. He didn't know where it was going, but he knew he had to adjust and play along to get Dominique to continue talking. Thornton had more questions—a lot more questions—and he needed answers.

"Well," the detective continued, "like I said, before you told us everything that happened with the ones we already talked about. But just to touch a little bit on the other ones we didn't talk about yet, let me ask you a question. You know where Highway Louisiana 347 is? You've been on that road before."

"In Lafourche," said Dominique.

"Like Kraemer Road?" Bergeron cut in.

"You've been on there before, you know what we're talking about, correct?" Thornton asked.

"You know where we're going?" Bergeron asked.

"What happened on Kraemer, Ronald?" Thornton said, the words coming at Dominique faster. "I know that there's a couple of things there."

"Just put my name on it, I don't care."

Reacting swiftly to the serial killer's self-pity, Bergeron declared, "No! We're not gonna charge you like that, and if you don't care, *we* care."

"I don't wanna talk about nothing no more. I'm tired," Dominique declared.

They still had a long way to go and a narrow window within which to do it. But a confession obtained while keeping a suspect without sleep or breaks could quickly be overturned by an appeals court. Besides, both cops played fair. It wasn't their style to abridge a suspect's constitutional rights, serial killer or not.

"You're really tired, alright?" said Thornton, acknowledging for the record the suspect's state of mind.

"Would you like to go get some sleep and let's come back and talk to you tomorrow?" Bergeron offered.

"I don't wanna talk no more. I'm tired. I just wanna go to sleep and I don't want to wake up."

Thornton and Bergeron knew they would have to put a suicide watch on him when he reached his cell. A guard would have to watch him constantly.

"Okay," Thornton said, "but you're gonna wake up tomorrow. When's the last time you slept?"

Dominique said nothing. Thornton, meanwhile, had been showing his concern by asking the question, but he had no intention of taking Dominique anywhere. They had to get him to open up more. Otherwise, they only had him for the two murders. That meant twenty-one to go.

"Were you sleeping today when we picked you up?" Bergeron asked.

"Off and on," Dominique finally answered. "My chest hurts too much to sleep. I haven't been sleeping since I had my first heart attack. There's too much pressure on my chest."

Thornton had a hunch.

"Did that pressure come from all this?" Thornton asked, meaning serial killing.

"No, I got stung by a wasp and I had a heart attack."

"No, I mean other than that."

They weren't medical doctors, but a wasp causing a heart attack made as much sense to the detectives as the black pepper story. Unless he was allergic to the venom.

"You think it was all the stress that built up?" Bergeron asked.

"No, it just hitted all at once."

"Okay, Ronald," said Thornton.

"I never had no problems," Dominique insisted. "I just got stung by the wasp and they found I had a blockage."

Thornton realized they needed to keep him focused on the killings.

"Well, here's a question for you. We talked about the last four last year and that's kind of, I don't mean to be rude here, okay, but that's kind of a busy year. How did you deal with that?"

Thornton really wanted to know what made the guy tick.

"I just kind of blocked it out and I didn't wanna remember nothing."

"What did you do for Hurricane Katrina? Did you stay?" asked Thornton.

"We went to stay at a friend's house the first hurricane, the second one we stayed at the trailer."

"But you came back eventually, right?"

"That was the last time."

"That was the last time?" Thornton repeated.

"Yes, sir," said Dominique.

"You didn't do anything since then?"

"No, 'cause I had my heart attack in September. I haven't messed with nobody."

Ironically, Dominique's ill health had probably spared someone's life.

"Did you try? Maybe try to pick somebody up and it just didn't work?" Bergeron asked.

"No," he answered promptly. Then he said that, after his heart attack, "most of the time my sister would do all the driving."

"Your sister?" asked Thornton.

There it was again: family problems. The detectives had no use for Dominique's whining. Thornton switched tactics and got more direct.

"Were you worried when you had them in your truck or your car about being stopped by the police?"

"Yes."

Thornton had finally gotten someplace; Bergeron wasted no time stepping in.

"Did you ever get stopped with anybody with you? Pulled over for anything?"

"I don't think so."

Thornton remembered the preliminary report of the forensic team. Could there be evidence in the trailer they had not yet found?

"Let me ask you this, Ronald," said Thornton casually. "In your trailer, in your RV, looking in there, is there anything that ever came off the guys you had there and stayed in there?"

"No," Dominique answered firmly.

"Just maybe they left any articles of clothing or jewelry?" Bergeron asked.

"No."

"Wallets?" asked Thornton.

"Shoes?" Bergeron wondered out loud, mindful of the old shoeless-killer angle.

"Shoes, identification, anything like that?" Thornton repeated.

"No."

Dominique was adamant; he was a different kind of serial killer, one who didn't keep souvenirs of the people he killed. Or so he claimed. A detailed search of his trailer might prove otherwise.

"Everything was thrown away," Dominique claimed.

If he had thrown away everything, including bindings and victims' clothing, there would be a distinct lack of physical evidence with which to further build their case. While he had already given a partial confession, there were many cases on record where an appeals court threw out a confession for lack of physical evidence to back it up.

"Everything—like what do you mean by that?" Bergeron cut in. "You said earlier that you threw some clothes away. What other types of items did you throw away? Jewelry?"

"Whatever they had."

"How about a driver's license? You ever thrown away a driver's license?" Thornton asked.

"Everything they had."

"Book sacks?" Bergeron said.

"Nobody brought a book sack."

It was true. The victims weren't honor students.

"Backpacks or anything like that? CD players?" Bergeron went on.

Some of the victims had had those items with them prior to their murders. Finding them in Dominique's trailer would link him conclusively to those murders. They needed strong, direct physical evidence.

Remembering the mode of transportation of many of the victims, Thornton leaned forward.

"What about a bicycle? You ever throw a bicycle away? Maybe once?"

"Maybe once or twice."

"Maybe once or twice," Thornton repeated, the words sounding pleasant to his ear. "Okay, let's say you're riding and there's a guy comes up to you on a bike and he wants to be with you. He don't leave his bike, right?"

"No."

"Can he put the bike in the back of your truck?" asked Thornton.

"I don't remember where I threw the bike."

"How many bikes did you get rid of?" asked Bergeron.

"Two."

Bergeron continued this line of questioning. "Where'd you throw the bikes, if you remember?"

"I think one of the bikes, the guy who I put in the mini-storage."

More specific information! Thornton grabbed for it.

"Okay, well, let's talk about the mini-storage. The guy you put in the mini-storage, he had a bike?" said Thornton.

"I think so."

"Where'd you put his bike?"

"I don't remember. I just remember throwing the bikes away someplace. You don't just drive down the street and toss it out."

That would attract attention. He had to find an isolated place to get rid of it instead.

"Did you go down a ways, and dump them in cane fields or the bayou?" said Bergeron.

"I think one of the bikes . . . the guy that I put in the mini-storage," Dominique answered.

He had thrown Michael Barnett's body in the storage unit.

"Who else had a bike?" Bergeron prodded. "Try to remember."

"I don't remember."

Yes, you do, Thornton thought.

"Do you remember a guy outside the mini-storage?"

"No."

"Like you could see the mini-storage?"

He was trying a visualization exercise with the serial killer. By using verbal clues, he was trying to re-create the scene.

"By the church, a little white church?" Bergeron asked.

"He was outside," Thornton added.

"If you pass the mini-storage and the pizza place, there's—"

"No," Dominique interrupted.

"—church on your right."

"I don't remember, I don't . . ."

His voice trailed off, but Thornton wasn't going to lose him.

"What about Kraemer?" referring to another victim picked up there.

"You remember that," added Bergeron.

Dominique sat there in his self-imposed silence. It was impossible to guess what was going on inside the serial killer's head. However, Bergeron and Thornton had him on a confessional roll. If they lost him now, they might not find him as cooperative again. Both detectives knew this.

"You remember, don't you?" Thornton nudged.

That brought no reply, so Bergeron switched tactics and tried the softer approach.

"What do you remember, Ronald? Tell us about it."

Thornton knew the use of Dominique's first name at that critical juncture would get him to open up. Maybe.

CHAPTER EIGHTEEN

CLEARING ALL TWENTY-THREE

"It's the same as the rest," Dominique finally answered.

Inwardly, Thornton breathed a sigh of relief. Bergeron bore in.

"How many?"

"One."

"What happened there?"

Dominique didn't remember the pickup, but he did remember dumping the body.

"On the side of the road by a fence."

"Black or white guy?" Bergeron asked.

"Black."

"You remember where you picked him up?"

"I don't wanna see no more pictures," Dominique whined.

"Just one more?"

"No."

"You said he was by a fence," Bergeron said. "Did you dump him on the left or right of it?"

"I don't remember."

"You do think you picked him up in Houma though, Ronald?"

"Yes."

That established the jurisdiction for the case. Since the crime itself began in Houma, Terrebonne Parish had venue.

"You remember the person by the fence?"

Thornton was talking about victim Michael Vincent, whose body was found draped over the barbed wire fence.

"I don't remember, I'm serious."

"Did you go anywhere else other than in your truck, or to the camper? A friend's house?" Bergeron asked.

"No."

"How many times you use handcuffs, Ronald?" she asked. "You ever use handcuffs?" Some killers could get very kinky.

"No."

"Did any of them wanna be handcuffed?" Thornton asked.

"I don't remember the faces."

"Okay, that's fair enough," Thornton said. "I understand if you don't remember the faces."

After all, twenty-three faces would be hard to remember.

"I told you all I remember is that I don't remember anything else. I don't!"

"Was there sex involved?" Bergeron asked.

"Yes."

"Okay, was there tying of the wrist? Of the feet?" she asked.

"Yes."

"Which one?"

"Both."

"Okay, I don't wanna put words in your mouth. You gotta fill in here. Tell me about the scene," she continued, mindful of the tape, the Constitution, and the opportunity to clear Vincent's homicide right here and now.

"I don't remember where."

"Were you in the RV or were you in the truck?"

"I don't remember. I don't."

Both Thornton and Bergeron could see Dominique was tired and turning uncooperative. They stopped the tape and stepped into the hall to determine if they should continue questioning him now or take him to his cell for some sleep and resume tomorrow. They needed to talk to him a little more off tape to help them decide.

The tape recorder went back on at 11:22 p.m. After a few of the usual formal preliminaries when a taped statement starts—stating the suspect's name, birth date, and names of the officers taking his statement—Thornton got down to brass tacks.

"Okay, Ronald, we'd like to ask you about one more incident where you indicated that in Lafourche Parish on LA 7, you remember placing a black male subject near a fence?"

"Yes."

"Is that correct?" Thornton repeated.

"Yes, sir."

"Okay, just tell us a little bit more. What do you remember about that incident?"

"We fooled around like the rest of them. Then he was gonna call the police and then after I strangled him, I dropped him off," Dominique answered, as nonchalantly as if he were taking out the trash.

"Let's talk about this. When you say 'fool around,' once again, we're talking about what? And in what vehicle was this?" Thornton asked.

"I don't remember where it was, or what was done in it."

"Were you using your truck at the time?"

"Yes, sir."

The black Sonoma. Dominique had now identified it as the vehicle he used to pick up his victims.

"This picture is labeled 'twenty,'" said Bergeron, handing him a picture of Wayne Smith, victim number twenty.

Dominique looked down at it with no emotion.

"Tell us about the person in this picture," she continued.

"Yes, I met him. I was living at my sister's house at the time."

"So you met this person, which has been identified as Wayne Smith. When did you meet him?"

"He flagged me down when I was passing. He was riding a bicycle."

"Where at?" Thornton asked.

"On the east side of Houma. I was in my black Sonoma."

So much for a mysterious white van.

"Okay, what happens?"

"He asked me if I was looking for drugs and I told him no. He asked me if I fool around and I told him yes. He said he does too. He went to drop off his bike. He told me to wait while he did that."

"Did he get in your truck when he came back?"

"Yes, ma'am."

"Where did you go?"

"The Dixie Shipyard, to my RV. It was my brother-in-law's, but he gave it to me."

He explained how his brother-in-law had gotten him access to the deserted shipyard. After he and Smith went inside his trailer, they got undressed.

"Did y'all have a discussion about what was gonna happen?" Bergeron continued.

"Yeah, I told him that I don't take it in the rectum and I was scared I would get raped."

"So what kind of arrangements were made?"

"I tied his hands, so he couldn't rape me. We're laying on the ground on the floor and give each other head. Then he goes on his stomach and tells me to put it in. And he starts saying he liked it. Then after we finish, he told me I had to pay him or he was gonna call the cops. I panicked and got nervous 'cause I don't wanna go to jail. So I started choking him."

"How'd you do that?" Thornton asked.

"With an extension cord. I stopped when I noticed he wasn't breathing. I tied him up and put him in my truck. I put his clothes back on too."

"So you put him in the GMC Sonoma?" Bergeron continued.

Dominique quickly answered yes. "I dropped him in a ditch on the side of the road."

Despite his lethargy, they had just gotten Dominique to confess to another murder. Thornton kept the pressure on.

"Okay, Ronald, we're going to move on just a little bit," said Thornton, "to another one."

Bergeron held up a mug shot of Michael Barnett.

"This is picture number fifteen. Where'd you meet him?"

"By the Mobil station on 182 in Houma next to the Sugar Bowl Motel."

The detectives glanced at each other. They had been right about the pickup site.

"I came out the store," Dominique continued, "and he approached me and said he needed to make some money to pay his boardinghouse. I told him all I had was twenty dollars. He said anything would help and I asked him what he was into. He said, 'Fooling around with guys.' So I brought him to the RV."

From there, it was business as usual, tying him up in preparation for sex and death.

"We sucked each other. Then he tells me I could put it in and after I do, he wants more money. I told him that was all I had. He said he would go to the police if I didn't give him more."

With his hands tied, it was easy for him to choke Michael Barnett to death. Once again, a body was placed in the back of the Sonoma and Dominique drove around, looking for a dump site. He drove by the pizza place and saw the storage units located nearby.

"What gave you the idea to put him there?" Thornton asked.

"I don't know, I was just scared. I just saw it."

It was convenient; an improvisation. Dominique was good at improvising, though this wasn't Second City. It was murder.

"I put him in, closed the door, got in my truck, and threw his clothes out the window. Don't remember where."

"Now, Ronald, we're going to move on to another face," Thornton said.

He showed Dominique a picture of Leon Lirette. It was the same story. Dominique claimed he waved Lirette down and asked him if he wanted to make a few dollars. Lirette did.

"What happened next?" asked Bergeron.

"We talked for a while and I told him I was getting kind of scared 'cause I got raped in prison. He started rubbing my shoulder, telling me everything was going to be alright. Then he got in the truck and we went to the RV. He was already almost half-dressed, 'cause he had his pants hanging off his butt and he just started undressing."

"Did you tie him up?" Bergeron asked, knowing the answer.

"These guys, all they want is money," Dominique said in frustration.

"The RV, where was it parked?" Thornton asked.

"At the shipyard."

They needed more specific information, the kind that would be included in Dominique's murder indictments.

"Was it the same place where you brought the other three you just told us about? Yes or no?" Thornton asked.

"Yes," Dominique answered.

He went on to describe how he choked Lirette with an extension cord. Then he put his clothes back on.

"I brought him by the air base and dropped him off."

Thornton looked down at the cassette.

"Okay, we're gonna take a short break. Stop the tape."

When he said short break, Thornton meant it. He turned the tape over and then turned the recorder back on.

It was important to document Dominique's MO again for the indictment. They needed to give the parish district attorney everything possible to gain a conviction.

"Do they ever ask for money in advance?"

"I usually put it on the side. Like on the bed thing where they could see it. After we finish fooling around, he told me he wanted three hundred bucks and I told him I didn't have that much, that all I had was thirty dollars."

"Is he still tied at this point?" asked Bergeron.

"Yes, ma'am. He told me that he was gonna go to the cops."

So he had no choice but to strangle him and get rid of the body.

"I just panicked," Dominique confessed. "I was scared that they wouldn't believe my story and they'd bring me to jail."

"When they're tied up and you're having sex with them, before they even say something you don't like, do they ever tell you, 'Hey, untie me?'"

"No, 'cause they wanna hurry up and get it over with so they can get their money."

"Alright, when he tells you that he's gonna go to the police, can he see you?" Thornton asked, regarding Lirette.

"No, he's face down. I just hold the extension cord and put it around his neck."

Bergeron noted it was the second time an extension cord was mentioned as a method of execution.

"Do you wrap it all the way around, Ronald?"

"I just pull it around," Dominique said simply.

"Everything you're stating here has been truthful and to the best of your knowledge?"

"Yes."

And the recorder was turned off.

They could see he was hungry. Dominique had something to eat. They allowed him some time to rest and then, once again, they brought him into the interview room and turned the tape on. It was still just Thornton and Bergeron; their superiors and the other detectives who were part of the task force were watching through the two-way glass, hearing everything thanks to a microphone secreted in the interview room.

They had established their rapport; had anyone else come in, there was a good chance Dominique would clam up. Thornton continued.

"Okay, Ronald, you are aware we've been talking to you about some incidents involving your encounters with black male subjects that you've agreed to talk about, is that correct?"

"Yes."

"Okay, tell us a little bit about the guy at the fence."

"I just remember we fooled around. Like the rest of them, he was gonna call the police and then after I strangled him, I dropped him off."

"Where?"

"The fence on LA 7."

"Do you remember if he had clothes on or not?" asked Bergeron.

"I don't remember."

"What kind of fence was it?"

"I think it was a barbed wire fence. They had a lot of barbed wire there."

"Now, Ronald, I know you're trying hard, but is there something in your mind that stands out about him?" Thornton asked.

"I don't remember."

Once again, Dominique was getting tired and less cooperative. This looked like the time to take a real break.

"Can you think of anything else, Ronald?"

"No, sir."

The tape was turned off at 11:29 p.m.

That night, while Dominique slept in his cell, Thornton and Bergeron had a conversation with Terrebonne Parish's district attorney.

Dominique had talked a lot, enough to up his indictment from two murders to all eight of the men from Terrebonne Parish. That left another fifteen that they knew he was also responsible for killing. Still, the detectives were excited and relieved that their serial killer had confessed.

No longer would Ronald J. Dominique be able to roam the bayous searching for victims to strangle. Thornton and Bergeron had nailed him good! But now they needed to be looking forward, toward indictment and prosecution. They did, conferring with Terrebonne Parish district attorney Mark Rhodes. He would be prosecuting Dominique.

They talked long into the night about how to proceed. After all these years of investigating him and not knowing who he was, they finally had their serial killer behind bars and he wasn't going anyplace but court.

They knew that if the state sought the death penalty against Dominique, he would have no incentive to continue cooperating. They wanted to clear all twenty-three murders and give much-needed closure to the victims' families. A joint decision was reached to make a deal with Dominique. It was simple.

The next day, he was to lead them to all twenty-three dump sites.

If he would do that, and plead guilty to eight of the murders, they would give him a life sentence. They couldn't make all the cases airtight, but that wasn't the point. The point was to bring closure to the families of the deceased while punishing Dominique. For him, it was a much better deal than going to Louisiana's death chamber. Damn good deal!

CHAPTER NINETEEN

THE COCKEYED CARAVAN

It didn't take long for Dominique to agree to the deal. Despite his protestations to the contrary, he wanted to live. Patti Labelle impersonation aside, the guy did tend to be a little dramatic about wanting to cash it all in.

The next morning began one of the strangest road trips in American criminal history. About half a dozen unmarked police cars containing detectives and forensic specialists began the somber ride through the bayou.

"We organized a caravan," said Thornton. "We had Dominique take us to the places where he dumped the bodies. He remembered the locations. We wanted him to take us and not the other way around."

With good reason. They didn't want a smart defense lawyer saying they had put words in the suspect's mouth, or thoughts in his head, for that matter; that they set him up in some way to admit guilt to murders he didn't actually commit. They had him for all twenty-three—*if* things went right. Twenty-three individuals who were fathers, brothers, uncles; twenty-three men whose families were still coping with their loved ones' deaths.

If Dominique were a nineteenth-century gunslinger, he would have twenty-three notches on his gun.

All day on December 2, 2006, from morning till night, the cockeyed caravan wound its way silently through the Southern Louisiana parishes to all twenty-three dump sites. Dominique had a new role; he was their tour guide through hell and back. Thornton and Bergeron were tired from the questioning, but anxious to make the cases. And now they were trying once more to speak for the dead.

Driving through the parishes, Dominique pointed out the dump sites from the car. Sometimes, they would take the hand-cuffed killer out of the car, and have him point something out or approach a dump site. Then he would lumber forward. At no time did he show any remorse, absolutely no emotion about what he had done. He appeared to be the very definition of a sociopath.

The detectives knew Dominique was telling the truth about murdering all twenty-three men because only the killer would have such exact knowledge of the dump sites, where evidence of the murders had been collected by the forensic teams. Dominique didn't talk much; he would just point out the places, and the police and techies would examine them.

By the end of the day, they had gone to all twenty-three body-dump sites. That is a lot of grief. Dominique's memories echoed inside Thornton's own head. He had seen it from the other side: he had felt the cop's frustration at identifying the victims soon after they were murdered. Now that he was finally bringing them justice, Thornton felt an intense sense of relief.

The detectives still had a tremendous amount of work to do. When the caravan arrived back at the Terrebonne Parish Sheriff's Office, Thornton and Bergeron hustled the handcuffed, confessed killer back into the interview room. Before they went in, they agreed that it was time to clear up a few details that had been bothering both of them. To get Dominique to open up this time, they would give him his say on things and in the process, get what they wanted.

Going inside the room, the detectives sat down, once again across from Dominique, who sat in his chair, hands still cuffed. He showed no expression, except perhaps for indifference. Thornton turned on the tape recorder.

"Well, Ronald, what else do you wanna talk about?"

Now that is a great opening line.

"I'm not a bad person," Dominique insisted. "When I was younger, I was molested twice. I've been teased by family members and people that was supposed to be friends. I was accused by two people of raping them and it wasn't true. I had to serve time in jail. I got beat up when I was there, for no reason, by a person that killed somebody.

"I proved I was innocent and I got out. I was angry. I did something to some of the guys and then I got raped by a guy and I protected myself and I killed him and then another one tried to rape me and stab me and I killed him. I took all the anger out on the rest of the guys and I shouldn't have took it out on them. I know I took them from their family and hurt their family."

Sounded good, but Thornton and Bergeron knew better. The guy killed twenty-three individuals deliberately and he wasn't a bad person? Any pain he felt was learned. That's what sociopaths do: they learn emotions; they don't feel them.

"That I should've seeked help, but I didn't know how and I'm very sorry."

The detectives didn't have to say what was on their mind. "Sorry" isn't going to bring your victims back. Instead, Thornton asked him if there was anything else he wanted to add, maybe talk a little bit more about his anger? Maybe he could tell the detectives what made him so angry that he had to kill continuously?

It wasn't necessarily important for the indictment, but for a detective it was invaluable information on what made a killer go way over the top. This was a unique opportunity to understand what motivated the worst serial killer of the new millennium to go out trolling for other human beings to murder.

"People call me a fag, queer, and all kinds of stuff that's not called for," said Dominique firmly.

"And you're forty-two years old, right?" Bergeron asked.

"Yes."

"Okay, when all this was going on, who would call you those words?"

"Nephews, friends."

"Your family?" Bergeron said.

"My family, some of them," Dominique answered readily.

Bergeron was doing an absolutely brilliant job building rapport with the serial killer.

"And what is your sexual preference?"

"First, I tried to get married," he answered. "They teased me and that didn't work. So I couldn't bring nobody home 'cause I was scared they'd tell them, 'What are you doing with a queer?' Then after that, they called me queer *and* a fag."

"When did they start picking on you?" asked Bergeron.

"It seems like it's been forever."

"Did they pick on you when you were younger?"

"My little brother used to call me things. He used to do things and my mama always took up for him and blamed me."

"When you were younger, did your family know you were gay?" asked Thornton.

"I don't remember exactly when, but probably before I was twenty."

"And it was a rough time in jail?" chimed in Bergeron.

"Yes."

He said that he had been raped in prison, that he was never going back.

"When you got out, is that when all this other stuff started?" Bergeron asked.

"Yes, 'cause I was angry, because I didn't do it and I was put in jail and treated bad and was beaten," Dominique continued, his voice breaking.

"And you were still being picked on when you were doing this?" Thornton said, referring to the murders.

"Yes, by family members."

"People you lived with?"

"No. There's only one sister I lived with. She don't. But her son picks on me, her daughter's husband picks on me, and her son's friends call me all kind of things."

"You obviously told them to stop," said Thornton sympathetically.

"It don't help."

Thornton didn't speculate that Dominique's persecution complex was part of what propelled him to kill. Neither did Bergeron. That wasn't their job. Their job was to get the entire truth, and get their conviction. Dominique claimed the killings were justified, on the pretense that the victims would report him to the police. They knew that wasn't true.

"You indicated earlier that a lot of these men, or all of them, you picked them up and took them back to your trailer. They wanted you or they were gonna have sex with you. They were gonna go to the police. They wanted more money. That's not totally true, is it?" Thornton demanded.

"Yes."

The cops had it right; Dominique had been lying all along.

"Some of them were straight and some of them wasn't," Dominique continued. "Some of them I picked up by showing them a picture of a girl. I asked them if they wanted to fool around with the girl. I told them that the girl had got hurt, raped, and they had to be tied up before she comes over. But it wasn't true."

"How many guys did you use that picture on that got into the truck with you?" Bergeron asked.

"I'll say six or seven."

Translation: six or seven of his victims were straight.

"It didn't matter to you whether they were straight or not?" Thornton said.

"No, I was just mad. I just took it out and I had no reason."

"And they would think they would get the girl if you tied them up?"

"Yes. After they was tied, I told them it wasn't true, it was me."

Thornton caught Bergeron's eye and they both thought the same thing. When Dominique told the victims the truth, they knew they were in trouble.

"Either they thought they was gonna have sex with a woman for money, or with me for money."

"But in essence, all of them got what type of sex?" said Thornton.

"Raped," Dominique finally admitted.

"Against their will?" Bergeron asserted.

"Yes."

"And then what'd they get?" Thornton asked.

"Strangled," said Dominique simply.

Bergeron thought about it. Some of the victims must have shouted, or at least tried to, and Dominique would have stopped it in some way. She asked the killer if anything was shoved in the victims' mouths to keep them quiet.

"A towel if they hollered."

That would explain how any of the victims he murdered at his sister's house who did try to scream out could not be heard. Dominique had been very, very smart.

"Are you glad it's stopping?" Thornton wondered out loud.

"Yes," Dominique answered. "Just as soon as we got to the camper, they took off their clothes and I start taking mine off and things just happened."

If they didn't want to be tied up, he'd just let them go. He was not crazy. He knew that if they were not immobilized, he could not kill them without a struggle. The last thing he wanted was for a potential victim to run out of the trailer naked and call the cops. After his encounter with parolee John Banning, who got away, Banning's parole officer had talked to him at Bergeron and Thornton's request, which had finally led to identifying Dominique as the serial killer.

"What else do you have to say, Ronald?" said Thornton.

"I just want everybody to forgive me. I'm sorry; I didn't mean to."

He sounded like he meant it. But even if he was capable of remorse, it was much too late.

"Okay, Ronald, everything you stated here is truthful to the best of your knowledge?" Thornton added.

"Yes."

"This statement is now ended. It's December 3, 2006. It's 2:53 a.m. End of statement," said Thornton, and Bergeron turned the tape recorder off.

EPILOGUE

Terrebonne Parish, September 24, 2008

Assistant District Attorney Mark Rhodes of Terrebonne Parish had drawn up Ronald J. Dominique's case. Richard Goorley of the Capital Assistance Center of Louisiana represented Dominique. Within two years of his arrest—which is not a lot of time in a capital murder case, let alone one involving twenty-three victims in numerous parishes—they made a deal.

The idea was to get Dominique off the streets. And his statement wasn't enough to convict him on twenty-three counts of murder without forensics to back up each one.

Now, lots of things can happen to serial killers who avoid the death chamber and get life instead. Albert DeSalvo, a.k.a. the Boston Strangler, was murdered by another inmate when he was in general population. Same thing happened to Jeffrey Dahmer. So who's to say what prisoners at Angola would do to Dominique once they got a hold of him?

Rhodes and Goorley made their deal: Ronald J. Dominique would plead guilty to the eight counts of murder on which the state figured they had him over the proverbial barrel. Rhodes told all the victims' families that while he was confident he could get a guilty verdict on all eight counts, he was equally confident it would be tied up in appeals for twelve or fifteen years or more if they charged him with all twenty-three murders.

It was better to make the deal.

In court, Dominique sat at the defense table. Shackled at the feet and waist, he was hunched over, exposing his close-cropped and sparse gray hair. Bergeron and Thornton, who were in the courtroom for the sentencing, noticed that Dominique had been dressed for the occasion by the county in an ill-fitting white jumpsuit.

District Judge Randy Bethancourt began by asking Dominique a series of questions to ascertain if he was aware that his plea of guilty for the murders of eight men meant that he was going to jail for life. Then the judge read the eight names.

"Kenneth Randolph, Michael Barnett, Leon Lirette, August Watkins, Kurt Cunningham, Alonzo Hogan, Chris DeVille, Wayne Smith, Nicholas Pellegrin."

Not once did Dominique look up, keeping his head down in an intense examination of the courtroom's floor. Then it was Assistant District Attorney Mark Rhodes's turn. He brought his A game to the sentencing.

"The lives of eight young men were taken from these families by the actions of the defendant," Rhodes told the court. "He knew nothing about them or their families and he callously killed the victims and left a lifetime of pain as their legacy."

Thirty relatives of the victims were in the courtroom, wrapping arms around one another in grief. Before pronouncing the sentence it was time for the victims' impact statements. Some came forward.

"I hope he burns in hell, pretty much. I hope the man burns in hell. I'm sure he will," Chris Cunningham told the judge of his brother Kurt's killer. Then he addressed Dominique directly, who refused to look at him. "I'll miss him to the day I die," he continued, sobbing. "I hope hell finds you fast!"

Then it was Cynthia Barabin's turn. She is the sister of Chris DeVille.

"The nature of what he did, and how he left my brother's body in a cane field for rodents to eat at him," she told the court. "When we found him, he was nothing. He was nothing but bones. Nothing. We had to bury bones."

Wayne Smith's mother wrote a letter to the court that was read aloud.

"It's been three years and I haven't seen my baby yet," Angela Smith wrote. "I put something in the ground, and I really don't know if my child is dead or not, because I did not get a chance to see my baby."

Judge Bethancourt offered Dominique a chance to make a statement before sentencing. He declined. Bethancourt then sentenced him to eight life sentences, to be served consecutively. That meant he would never see another day on the outside. Dominique did not respond. After the judge pronounced the sentence, Dominique, shackled and cuffed, was taken out of the courtroom to begin serving his time.

He did, indeed, make a very good deal.

Dominique's sister refused comment.

Dennis Thornton and Dawn Bergeron were both given promotions to detective captains, though neither ever expects to see something like Ronald J. Dominique again. But to remember what they did in saving lives and getting him, Bergeron, who now goes by her married name of Foret, kept a photo of her and Thornton and the other members of the task force in a frame on her desk.

In Houma, there are many people in town who have still never even heard of Ronald J. Dominique. They couldn't care less about him, or his victims. On the national stage, the story of Dominique's confession and conviction barely rated headlines outside the South. Though in Europe, they ate it up.

And Dominique? Now fifty-two years old, he resides in the general prison population of the Louisiana State Prison in Angola, where he will be for the rest of his life.

Ronald J. Dominique's trailers parked in
the police impound lot.

The Shriner's Hall, near which Dominique dumped a body.

One victim was found in this ditch at the end of a dead end road.

A cheap hotel in Terrebonne Parrish, where
Dominique went trolling for victims.

Mug shot of Ronald J.
Dominique. *(Courtesy of
Terrebonne Parrish Sheriff's
Office)*

A poster prepared by the sheriff's office featuring all of
Dominique's victims. *(Courtesy of Terrebonne Parrish Sheriff's Office)*

Ronald J. Dominique during questioning.
(Courtesy of Terrebonne Parrish Sheriff's Office)

Spec book cover painting by Raymond Gray.

The members of the serial killer task force that tracked
Dominique down. *(Courtesy of Dawn Bergeron)*

ACKNOWLEDGMENTS

This book, and a full accounting of Dominique's crimes, would not have been possible without Dawn Bergeron. When I flew out to Terrebonne Parish to meet her, she took me to all the dump sites. I got to see firsthand how Dominique operated. Not only did she give me access to all the official records of the case, she took me to the impound yard that held the trailers Dominique lived and killed in. I even got to go inside them.

We went to lunch one day at a local restaurant where, by coincidence, there were other cops from the parish. They ordered French-fried alligator and had me taste it, probably figuring I'd gag.

"Tastes like chicken," I said with a straight face, and we all laughed.

Dennis Thornton sat for one very long interview at Louis Armstrong New Orleans International Airport, which took the entertainer's name in 2001. Captain Thornton gave freely of his time with incredible details of the case and his involvement in it.

Philip Rappaport did a bang-up editing job! Nicole Passage, Lauren Chomiuk, and Connor McDonald continued the process of getting the manuscript ready for publication. Jaime Wolf gave his legal advice and perspective.

Dan Zupansky and Maria Sblendorio Ibrahim encouraged me greatly. Barbara Scott Tompkins befriended me when I needed it.

And then there's Scott Forbes. He was a handsome, struggling British actor in Hollywood when, in the late 1950s, he was cast by Desilu in *The Adventures of Jim Bowie*. He gave a very young Jewish boy from Brooklyn a Louisiana hero for life.

Throughout the writing of this book and for all those I have authored for the past twelve years, my best friend, Sammy, a loving Brittany, was by my side. One day after his birthday, as I was finishing the final copyedit, he died from canine cognitive dysfunction. God bless my Sammy Doodle!

If there is one thing about this case that I will never forget, it is the support I got from my daughter, Sara, who was in eighth grade when this book began.

"Good luck, Daddy," she said as she boarded the school bus while I took off for the airport and Louisiana.

While I was in Houma, Sara received an academic award from her school. It was the first time I had ever missed a school function. Right then and there, I understood the personal sacrifices Bergeron and Thornton had to endure to bring Dominique to justice.

ABOUT THE AUTHOR

Fred Rosen has written and published twenty-five books. His twenty-fifth, *Murdering the President: Alexander Graham Bell and the Race to Save James Garfield* (University of Nebraska Press, 2016), changes American history. Through his original research and detective work, Rosen proves Charles Guiteau didn't assassinate President Garfield, and uncovers who his real murderer was. Hank Garfield, the president's great-great-grandson, wrote the foreword.

Rosen is a brand name in true crime. He is the author of *Lobster Boy*, described by the *Guardian* newspaper as a "true crime masterpiece." His other true-crime books published by Open Road include *Body Dump*, *Needle Work*, *Gang Mom*, *The Mad Chopper*, *Deacon of Death*, *Blood Crimes*, *Gold!*, and *Did They Really Do It?*.

Rosen appears regularly as a commentator on Investigation Discovery programming, including *Evil Kin* and *Evil Twins*. He has also been on *Dateline NBC*. A former columnist for the

New York Times, he was an assistant professor of journalism at Hofstra University. Professor Rosen has a master of fine arts in cinema from the legendary film school at the University of Southern California.

He can be contacted through his Facebook email and welcomes correspondence with his readers.

FRED ROSEN

FROM OPEN ROAD MEDIA

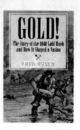

OPEN ROAD
INTEGRATED MEDIA

OPEN ROAD

INTEGRATED MEDIA

Find a full list of our authors and
titles at www.openroadmedia.com

FOLLOW US
@OpenRoadMedia